SWEETS
CAKE
SAY
yes
NO
try!

www.booksbyboxer.com

Bee Three Publishing is an imprint of Books By Boxer
Published by
Books By Boxer, Leeds, LS13 4BS, UK
Books by Boxer (EU), Dublin, D02 P593, IRELAND
Boxer Gifts LLC, 955 Sawtooth Oak Cir, VA 22802, USA

cs@boxer.gifts

MADE IN CHINA
ISBN: 9781915410801

MIX
Paper | Supporting responsible forestry
FSC™ C007683
FSC www.fsc.org

This book is produced from responsibly sourced paper to ensure forest management

WHISKEY AND RYE SALTED CARAMEL APPLE PIE

PREP TIME: 15 MINS **COOK TIME:** 40 MINS **SERVES:** 8

A HEAVENLY WHISKEY AND RYE TINGED PIE THAT DESERVES TO BE ON YOUR TABLE THIS THANKSGIVING!

FOR THE PIE:

- 200G | 7 OZ PLAIN FLOUR, PLUS EXTRA FOR DUSTING
- 100G | 3.5 OZ WHOLEMEAL RYE FLOUR
- 2 TBSP CASTER SUGAR
- 250G | 8.8 OZ UNSALTED BUTTER, DICED INTO 1CM PIECES
- 2 TBSP WHISKEY
- 1 EGG YOLK, BEATEN WITH 1 TBSP WATER (FOR GLAZING)
- DEMERARA SUGAR, FOR SPRINKLING

FOR THE SYRUP:

- 200G | 7 OZ CASTER SUGAR
- 35G | 1.2 OZ UNSALTED BUTTER
- A LARGE PINCH FLAKY SEA SALT
- 180ML | 6.1 OZ DOUBLE CREAM

FOR THE FILLING:

- 3 LARGE GRANNY SMITH APPLES PEELED AND SLICED
- 3 LARGE BRAEBURN APPLES
- 1/2 LEMON, JUICED
- 2 TBSP LIGHT BROWN SUGAR
- 4 TBSP CORNFLOUR
- 1/2 TBSP GROUND CINNAMON
- 1/2 TBSP GROUND GINGER

METHOD

STEP 1 IN A MEDIUM PAN, GENTLY HEAT SUGAR UNTIL MELTED. BRING TO A BOIL UNTIL CARAMELIZED TO A RUSTY COLOR, SWIRLING CONSTANTLY. NEXT, ADD AND COMBINE BUTTER AND SALT. ADD CREAM CAREFULLY, ONE HALF AT A TIME. MIX IN, THEN WHEN BUBBLING SUBSIDES AND CARAMEL IS SMOOTH, REMOVE FROM HEAT, POUR INTO A CONTAINER AND CHILL.

STEP 2 ADD FLOURS, SUGAR, AND 1 TSP SALT INTO A LARGE BOWL AND MIX. ADD 1/4 OF THE BUTTER, RUB INTO MIXTURE WITH HANDS UNTIL BREADCRUMB-LIKE. ADD REMAINING BUTTER, COAT IN THE FLOUR, THEN PRESS EACH PIECE OF BUTTER FLAT. FREEZE FOR 20 MINS.

STEP 3 MIX THE WHISKEY WITH 6 TBSP OF ICE-COLD WATER. REMOVE DOUGH FROM FREEZER AND POUR WHISKEY MIXTURE OVER, STIRRING TO FORM A SHAGGY DOUGH. FLOUR THE SURFACE, THEN ROLL THE DOUGH INTO A LONG RECTANGLE (6X15-INCH APPROX). ROLL INTO A THICK SAUSAGE, CUT INTO TWO PIECES. MAKE BOTH DOUGHS INTO TWO FLAT DISCS, WRAP IN PLASTIC WRAP THEN CHILL FOR AN HOUR.

STEP 4 MIX APPLES WITH LEMON JUICE, BROWN SUGAR, CORNFLOUR, CINNAMON, AND GINGER.

STEP 5 TAKE ONE DOUGH DISC AND ROLL OUT ON A LIGHTLY FLOURED SURFACE UNTIL ABOUT 1/8 OF AN INCH, AND A FEW INCHES LARGER THAN THE PIE TIN. ROLL DOUGH ONTO THE ROLLING PIN, THEN UNROLL INTO THE PIE TIN, TRIMMING THE EDGES TO ABOUT 1 INCH. CHILL IN THE FRIDGE. REPEAT WITH THE SECOND DOUGH BUT CUT INTO STRIPS AROUND AN INCH WIDE.

STEP 6 GET THE PIE TIN OUT OF THE FRIDGE, AND LAYER THE APPLES AND CARAMEL. RESERVE 1/3 OF THE CARAMEL.

STEP 7 EVENLY PLACE HORIZONTAL STRIPS ACROSS THE PIE, LEAVING SPACE BETWEEN. LAY A SINGLE STRIP VERTICALLY DOWN THE CENTRE OF THE PIE, LIFTING EVERY OTHER VERTICAL STRIP UP AND OVER. NOW FOLD BACK THE ALTERNATE HORIZONTAL STRIPS, AND PLACE YOUR NEXT VERTICAL STRIP DOWN BEFORE FOLDING BACK OVER. REPEAT ALTERNATELY UNTIL THE PIE IS COVERED IN A LATTICE EFFECT.

STEP 8 TRIM THE EDGES. ROLL EXCESS PASTRY INTO A SAUSAGE AND PLACE ON THE RIM OF THE TIN, AND CRIMP THE EDGES. BRUSH WITH BEATEN EGG YOLK, SPRINKLE WITH SUGAR, AND CHILL FOR 30 MINS.

STEP 9 HEAT THE OVEN TO 200 C / 392 F, AND BAKE FOR 15 MINS. REDUCE TEMPERATURE TO 180 C / 355 F AND BAKE FOR AN HOUR, UNTIL DEEP GOLDEN BROWN WITH A BUBBLING FILLING. COOL SLIGHTLY THEN SERVE WITH THE SALTED CARAMEL. ENJOY!

MOJITO CAKE

PREP TIME: 20 MINS **COOK TIME:** 40 MINS **SERVES:** 10

A FRESH AND ZESTY CAKE INSPIRED BY YOUR FAVORITE TROPICAL COCKTAIL.

FOR THE CAKE:

- 225G | 8 OZ SOFTENED SALTED BUTTER
- 225G | 8 OZ GOLDEN CASTER SUGAR
- 4 LARGE EGGS
- 225G | 8 OZ SELF-RAISING FLOUR
- ZEST OF 2 LIMES
- 50G | 2 OZ NATURAL YOGURT

FOR THE SYRUP:

- 3 LIMES JUICED
- 100G | 3.5 OZ LIGHT BROWN SOFT SUGAR
- SMALL BUNCH MINT LEAVES PICKED AND ROUGHLY CHOPPED
- 120ML | 4 OZ WHITE RUM

FOR THE BUTTERCREAM:

- 150G | 2 OZ SOFTENED UNSALTED BUTTER
- 400G | 14.5 OZ POWDERED SUGAR
- ZEST OF 2 LIMES
- 50G | 2 OZ CREAM CHEESE

METHOD

STEP 1 ADD THE BUTTER AND SUGAR INTO A LARGE MIXING BOWL AND BEAT UNTIL FLUFFY. WHISK IN YOUR EGGS AND ONCE COMBINED ADD THE FLOUR, GRATED LIME ZEST, AND YOGURT.

STEP 2 DIVIDE THE MIXTURE EVENLY INTO TWO PRE-GREASED 20CM / 8-INCH ROUND CAKE TINS. BAKE IN THE CENTRE OF A PREHEATED OVEN FOR 25-30 MINS AT 180 C / 355 F, TURNING ONTO WIRE RACKS ONCE FINISHED BAKING.

STEP 3 MAKE THE SYRUP TO POUR OVER YOUR CAKES. ADD HALF OF THE LIME JUICE AND ALL OF THE SUGAR AND MINT LEAVES TO A SAUCEPAN AND BRING TO THE BOIL (YOU MAY NEED TO ADD WATER TO HELP THE SUGAR DISSOLVE). THIS SHOULD GENTLY BUBBLE FOR AROUND 8 MINUTES - REMOVE FROM THE HEAT AND SLOWLY ADD THE RUM AND REMAINING LIME JUICE. LEAVE TO INFUSE AND COOL FOR 10 MINUTES. ONCE COOLED PRICK YOUR CAKES WITH A TOOTHPICK AND SLOWLY POUR OVER YOUR MOJITO SYRUP.

STEP 4 NOW MAKE THE BUTTERCREAM, BY BEATING TOGETHER THE BUTTER, ICING SUGAR, AND LIME ZEST UNTIL FLUFFY - YOU MAY WANT TO USE AN ELECTRIC WHISK FOR THIS! THEN ADD YOUR CREAM CHEESE UNTIL JUST COMBINED. USE THE BUTTERCREAM TO FILL YOUR TWO LAYERS AND SPREAD AROUND THE OUTSIDE OF THE CAKE.

STEP 5 DECORATE WITH MINT LEAVES AS WELL AS LIME ZEST AND WEDGES, AND ENJOY!

SELF SAUCING WHISKEY PUDDING

PREP TIME: 10 MINS **COOK TIME:** 35 MINS **SERVES:** 3

RICH AND INDULGENT, THIS SELF-SAUCING CHOCOLATE PUDDING IS PERFECT FOR CHRISTMAS.

FOR THE CAKE:

- 30G | 1 OZ SOFTENED UNSALTED BUTTER
- 60ML | 1/4 CUP MILK
- 1 EGG
- 1/2 TSP VANILLA EXTRACT
- 50G | 1/4 CUP GRANULATED SUGAR
- 60G | 1/2 CUP ALL-PURPOSE FLOUR
- 15G | 1/8 CUP COCOA POWDER
- 1/2 TSP BAKING POWDER
- PINCH OF SALT

FOR THE TOPPING:

- 50G | 1/4 CUP GRANULATED SUGAR
- 15G | 1/8 CUP COCOA
- 120ML | 1/2 CUP FRESHLY BOILED WATER
- 3 TBSPS WHISKEY OR DARK RUM, OPTIONAL

METHOD

STEP 1 PREHEAT THE OVEN 170 C / 340 F. GREASE THE INSIDE OF THREE RAMEKINS THAT ARE 5 X 9 CM / 2 X 3.5 INCHES, AT LEAST (IF YOU DON'T HAVE RAMEKINS USE A 6 INCH BAKING DISH).

STEP 2 IN A LARGE MIXING BOWL, COMBINE THE MELTED BUTTER, MILK, EGG, AND VANILLA. STIR AND COMBINE WELL.

STEP 3 STIR IN THE GRANULATED SUGAR, THEN SIFT IN THE REST OF THE CAKE'S DRY INGREDIENTS. FOLD GENTLY TO COMBINE AND REMOVE ANY OF THE LUMPS. SPLIT THE BATTER BETWEEN THE RAMEKINS.

STEP 4 IN A SMALL MIXING BOWL, COMBINE THE DRY INGREDIENTS FOR THE SAUCE. SPRINKLE OVER THE BATTER IN THE RAMEKINS. THEN STIR TOGETHER THE HOT WATER AND WHISKEY, POURING THE MIXTURE OVER THE RAMEKINS EQUALLY.

STEP 5 PLACE THE RAMEKINS ONTO A LINED BAKING TRAY (IN CASE THE SAUCE SPILLS) AND BAKE FOR 20-25 MINUTES UNTIL A STICK COMES OUT CLEAN.

STEP 6 ALLOW THEM TO REST FOR A FEW MINUTES, THEN SERVE WITH CREAM OR ICE CREAM. ENJOY!

CARIBBEAN RUM CAKE

PREP TIME: 40 MINS **COOK TIME:** 1 HR 20 MINS
SERVES: 10 **SOAKING TIME:** 48 HOURS

SOAKED IN DELICIOUS SPICED RUM, THIS CARIBBEAN RUM CAKE IS SURE TO PACK A PUNCH!

FOR THE FRUIT BASE:

- 50G | 2 OZ DRIED PRUNES
- 65G | 2.5 OZ SULTANAS
- 25G | 1 OZ GLACÉ CHERRIES
- 50G | 2 OZ RAISINS
- 35G | 1.5 OZ MIXED PEEL
- 2 STICKS CINNAMON
- 150ML | 5.5 OZ SPICED RUM

FOR THE CAKE BASE:

- 225G | 8 OZ UNSALTED BUTTER
- 225G | 8 OZ DARK BROWN MUSCOVADO SUGAR
- 5 EGGS
- 1 TSP VANILLA EXTRACT
- ZEST OF 1 LEMON
- ZEST OF 1 ORANGE
- 150G | 5.5 OZ PLAIN FLOUR
- 25G | 1 OZ GROUND ALMONDS
- 1 TSP BAKING POWDER

BROWNING:

- 45ML | 1.5 OZ MOLASSES SYRUP OR SUGAR
- 45ML | 1.5 OZ SPICED RUM

SOAKING:

- 1000ML | 35 OZ SPICED RUM

METHOD

STEP 1 ADD ALL FRUIT BASE INGREDIENTS INTO A BOWL. POUR IN SPICED RUM AND MIX WELL TO COAT. PUT THE MIXTURE IN AN AIRTIGHT CONTAINER AND LEAVE TO SOAK FOR AT LEAST 48 HOURS. ONCE SOAKED, DISCARD THE CINNAMON STICKS AND BLEND THE FRUIT IN BLENDER UNTIL 3/4 SMOOTH.

STEP 2 PREHEAT THE OVEN TO 180 C / 360 F. BUTTER AND LINE A 20CM / 18-INCH SPRINGFORM TIN WITH PARCHMENT PAPER. IN A BOWL, CREAM THE BUTTER AND SUGAR TOGETHER UNTIL FLUFFY. IN A DIFFERENT BOWL, WHISK TOGETHER EGGS, VANILLA, ALMOND, AND CITRUS ZESTS. GRADUALLY POUR THE EGG MIXTURE INTO THE CREAMED MIXTURE, WHISKING LIGHTLY TO NOT KNOCK OUT THE AIR (DON'T WORRY IF IT CURDLES SLIGHTLY). SIFT THE FLOUR AND BAKING POWDER IN, ALONGSIDE THE ALMONDS. FOLD IN USING A METAL SPOON, KEEPING CARE TO RETAIN THE AIR. ADD THE BLENDED FRUIT MIX AND FOLD IN TO COMBINE. SET ASIDE.

STEP 3 IN A SMALL PAN, POUR IN THE MOLASSES AND SPICED RUM FOR BROWNING, THEN BRING TO A LOW BOIL. REDUCE THE HEAT AND COOK FOR 2-3 MINS UNTIL SYRUPY AND THE MIXTURE HAS REDUCED BY 1/3. QUICKLY POUR INTO THE CAKE MIXTURE AND MIX WELL.

STEP 4 POUR THE MIXTURE INTO THE TIN, LEVELING THE TOP WITH A KNIFE. BAKE FOR 1 HOUR 10 MINUTES OR UNTIL THE CAKE IS EVENLY DARK BROWN AND A STICK COMES OUT CLEAN. ALLOW TO COOL.

STEP 5 REMOVE THE CAKE FROM THE TIN (KEEPING THE PARCHMENT PAPER IN PLACE) AND PLACE ON A PLATE OR TRAY. USE A SKEWER TO POKE HOLES ACROSS THE SURFACE OF THE CAKE. SLOWLY POUR THE SOAKING RUM OVER THE CAKE, TAKING CARE TO FOCUS ON THE SKEWER HOLES. SERVE THE CAKE AND ENJOY!

PROSECCO VICTORIA SPONGE CAKE

PREP TIME: 35 MINS **COOK TIME:** 35 MINS **SERVES:** 10

WHAT DO YOU GET WHEN YOU COMBINE VICTORIA SPONGE, LEMON POUND CAKE, AND BUCK'S FIZZ?

FOR THE CAKE:

- 200G | 7 OZ UNSALTED BUTTER, PLUS EXTRA
- 200G | 7 OZ GOLDEN GRANULATED SUGAR
- 4 EGGS
- 175G | 6 OZ SELF-RAISING FLOUR
- 50G | 2 OZ GROUND ALMONDS
- 150ML | 5 OZ PROSECCO (OR SPARKLING WINE)
- 2 ORANGES, ZESTED AND JUICED
- 100G | 3.5G GRANULATED SUGAR
- GOLD SUGAR CRYSTALS

FOR THE FILLING:

- 300ML | 10 OZ DOUBLE CREAM
- 1 TSP VANILLA BEAN PASTE
- 1 TBSP ICING SUGAR
- 1 ORANGE, ZESTED AND 1 TBSP OF JUICE

METHOD

STEP 1 PREHEAT THE OVEN TO 180 C / 355 F. BUTTER AND LINE TWO 18CM / 7-INCH LOOSE-BOTTOMED TINS.

STEP 2 IN A BOWL, BEAT THE BUTTER AND SUGAR UNTIL LIGHT AND FLUFFY. ADD THE EGGS ONE AT A TIME, ADD THE FLOUR, ALMONDS, AND PINCH OF SALT, FOLDING TO COMBINE. FOLD IN 100ML / 3.5 OZ OF THE PROSECCO ALONGSIDE THE ORANGE ZEST, THEN DIVIDE THE MIXTURE BETWEEN THE TWO TINS, SMOOTHING THE TOPS. BAKE FOR 30-35 MINS UNTIL GOLDEN AND RISEN, THEN LEAVE TO COOL ON WIRE RACKS.

STEP 3 WHILST THE SPONGES ARE STILL SLIGHTLY WARM, POKE HOLES INTO THEM WITH A SKEWER. MIX TOGETHER THE ORANGE JUICE, GRANULATED SUGAR, AND 50ML / 1.5 OZ OF REMAINING PROSECCO, THEN POURING OVER THE SPONGES TO ABSORB. ALLOW TO COOL COMPLETELY.

STEP 4 IN A BOWL, WHIP TOGETHER ALL OF THE FILLING INGREDIENTS. WHEN SOFT PEAKS FORM, SPREAD BETWEEN THE TWO SPONGES AND SANDWICH TOGETHER. DUST WITH GOLDEN SUGAR AND SERVE. ENJOY!

APEROL CAKE

PREP TIME: 40 MINS **COOK TIME:** 1 HR 10 MINS **SERVES:** 10

AN ORANGEY ALMOND LOAF CAKE, WHICH WILL TRANSPORT YOU TO A ROOFTOP BAR SIPPING APEROL IN SUMMER.

FOR THE CAKE:

- 175G | 6.2 OZ BUTTER
- 225G | 7.9 OZ CASTER SUGAR
- 1 TBSP APEROL
- 1/8 TSP ALMOND EXTRACT
- ZEST OF 1 LARGE ORANGE AND 3 TBSP JUICE
- 2 MEDIUM EGGS (1 WHOLE, 1 SEPARATED)
- 250G | 8.8 OZ PLAIN FLOUR
- 75G | 2.6 OZ GROUND ALMONDS
- 2 MEDIUM EGG WHITES

FOR THE DRIZZLE:

- 5 TBSP APEROL
- 2 TBSP LEMON JUICE
- 125G | 4.4 OZ GRANULATED SUGAR

METHOD

STEP 1 PREHEAT THE OVEN TO 170 C / 340 F. BUTTER A 900G / 2 LB TIN AND LINE THE ENDS WITH A STRIP OF BAKING PAPER. IN A LARGE BOWL, MIX THE BUTTER, SUGAR, APEROL, ALMOND EXTRACT, ORANGE ZEST, AND JUICE, ALONGSIDE THE WHOLE EGG AND ONE YOLK, WITH AN ELECTRIC WHISK. WHEN VERY PALE AND FLUFFY, FOLD IN THE FLOUR AND GROUND ALMONDS.

STEP 2 CLEAN THE WHISK AND THEN IN A SEPARATE BOWL, WHISK THE REMAINING THREE EGG WHITES TO STIFF PEAKS.

STEP 3 ADD 1/3 OF THE EGG WHITES INTO THE BATTER TO LOOSEN, THEN GENTLY FOLD IN THE REST WITH A BIG METAL SPOON TO KEEP AS MUCH AIR AS POSSIBLE. SPOON INTO THE TIN AND LEVEL THE TOP. BAKE FOR 1 HOUR 10 MINS ON THE MIDDLE SHELF UNTIL RISEN AND A STICK COMES OUT CLEAN. IF NOT FULLY COOKED, RETURN FOR 10 MIN INCREMENTS.

STEP 4 WHEN THE CAKE IS OUT, POKE HOLES ALL OVER THE TOP OF THE CAKE USING A SKEWER. SPOON 2 TBSP OF APEROL OVER THE TOP. THEN MIX THE REMAINING APEROL WITH LEMON JUICE AND GRANULATED SUGAR, MIXING QUICKLY TO DISSOLVE. SPOON OVER TO COVER THE CAKE COMPLETELY. LEAVE IN TIN UNTIL COOL AND TOPPING IS SET, THEN SERVE AND ENJOY!

MARGARITA BALLS

PREP TIME: 30 MINS **SERVES:** 24

A FUN, SUGARY, AND ALCOHOLIC SNACK, EAT THESE ALONGSIDE A MARGARITA!

FOR THE MIXTURE :

- 1 PACKET OF VANILLA WAFERS
- 225G | 8 OZ BLANCHED ALMONDS, GROUND
- 225G | 8 OZ WHITE CHOCOLATE
- 60ML | 1/4 CUP TEQUILA
- 60 ML | 1/4 CUP ORANGE MARMALADE
- 2 TBSP LIGHT CORN SYRUP
- WHITE SUGAR TO COAT

METHOD

STEP 1 CRUSH THE VANILLA WAFERS INTO CRUMBS AND COMBINE WITH THE GROUND ALMONDS.

STEP 2 IN A MICROWAVE-SAFE BOWL, MELT THE WHITE CHOCOLATE IN 15 SECOND INTERVALS, STIRRING EACH TIME. MELT FOR 1-3 MINUTES OR ACCORDING TO INSTRUCTIONS.

STEP 3 COMBINE THE WET INGREDIENTS IN A BLENDER AND BLEND UNTIL SMOOTH.

STEP 4 ADD ALL 3 MIXTURES TOGETHER AND STIR. SHAPE INTO BALLS, COAT WITH THE SUGAR AND STORE IN THE FRIDGE. ENJOY!

SLOE GIN CAKE

PREP TIME: 25 MINS **COOK TIME:** 35 MINS **SERVES:** 12

RICH, FRUITY, AND AUTUMNAL, THIS LAYER CAKE IS SURE TO **WOW!**

FOR THE CAKE:

- 200G | 7 OZ BUTTER
- 200G | 7 OZ CASTER SUGAR
- 4 EGGS
- 175G | 6 OZ ALL-PURPOSE FLOUR
- 1 TSP BAKING POWDER
- 90G | 3 OZ GROUND ALMONDS
- 100ML | 3.5 OZ BUTTERMILK
- 4 TBSP FLAKED ALMONDS

FOR THE FILLING:

- 3.5 OZ | 100G BUTTER
- 140G | 5 OZ ICING SUGAR
- 3-4 DARK PURPLE PLUMS
- 150ML | 5 OZ SLOE GIN
- 30G | 1 OZ CASTER SUGAR

METHOD

STEP 1 PREHEAT THE OVEN TO 170 C / 340 F. IN A BOWL, CREAM THE BUTTER AND SUGAR UNTIL LIGHT AND FLUFFY, THEN ADD THE EGGS ONE AT A TIME AND BEAT THEM IN, EACH TIME ADDING 1 TBSP OF FLOUR AFTER. ADD THE REMAINING FLOUR, BAKING POWDER, AND GROUND ALMONDS AND GENTLY FOLD. THEN ADD THE BUTTERMILK AND FOLD AGAIN.

STEP 2 SPLIT THE MIXTURE BETWEEN TWO BUTTERED AND LINED 18CM / 7-INCH LOOSE-BASED SPONGE TINS. SPRINKLE THE ALMONDS OVER THE SURFACE. BAKE FOR 30-35 MINS OR UNTIL GOLDEN AND RISEN, THEN LEAVE TO COOL ON WIRE RACKS.

STEP 3 WHILST THE CAKE IS IN THE OVEN, BEAT UP THE BUTTER FOR FILLING UNTIL LIGHT AND CREAMY. THEN ADD THE ICING SUGAR AND BEAT IN.

STEP 4 IN A PAN, COOK TOGETHER THE PLUMS, SLOE GIN, AND SUGAR, UNTIL THE PLUMS HAVE SOFTENED BUT STILL HOLD SHAPE. SCOOP OUT THE PLUMS AND ALLOW TO COOL. FURTHER REDUCE THE LIQUID TO A SYRUP.

STEP 5 SPREAD THE BUTTERCREAM AND SOME OF THE SYRUP INBETWEEN THE TWO CAKES AND SANDWICH TOGETHER. DECORATE THE TOP OF THE CAKE WITH THE PLUMS, ALMONDS, AND ANOTHER DRIZZLE OF SYRUP. ENJOY!

BOURBON BLONDIES

PREP TIME: 10 MINS **COOK TIME:** 35 MINS **SERVES:** 12

DELICIOUS BOOZY, OAKY, VANILLA BLONDIES. WHAT COULD BE BETTER?

FOR THE MIXTURE :

- 1 STICK OF BUTTER
- 180G | 1 CUP BROWN SUGAR
- 1 EGG
- 1 TSP VANILLA
- 1/2 TSP FLAKY SALT
- 60ML | 1/4 CUP BOURBON
- 1/4 TSP BAKING POWDER
- 1 CUP | 120G + 1 TBSP ALL PURPOSE FLOUR

METHOD

STEP 1 PREHEAT OVEN TO 175 C / 350 F AND GREASE AN 20 X 20 CM / 8 X 8 INCH BAKING PAN.

STEP 2 MELT THE STICK OF BUTTER IN A MICROWAVE SAFE BOWL IN THE MICROWAVE, OR GENTLY IN A SAUCEPAN. ONCE MELTED, ALLOW TO COOL FOR A FEW MINUTES. WHISK IN THE BROWN SUGAR UNTIL COMPLETELY DISSOLVED.

STEP 3 THEN WHISK IN THE EGG, VANILLA, BOURBON, AND SALT.

STEP 4 USING A LARGE METAL SPOON OR SPATULA, GENTLY FOLD IN THE FLOUR AND BAKING SODA UNTIL WELL COMBINED.

STEP 4 BAKE IN THE OVEN FOR 35-40 MINS. LET COOL IN THE PAN FOR 10 MINS, THEN ON A WIRE RACK. CUT INTO SMALL SQUARES AND SERVE, ENJOY!

TEQUILA SUNRISE CAKE

PREP TIME: 20 MINS **COOK TIME:** 1 HR **SERVES:** 10

UNASSUMING ON THE OUTSIDE, COLORFUL ON THE INSIDE, THIS MAKES THE PERFECT PARTY CAKE!

FOR THE CAKE:

- 280G | 1 1/4 CUPS UNSALTED BUTTER
- 400G | 2 CUPS GRANULATED SUGAR
- 2 TBSP GRATED ORANGE ZEST
- 1 TSP VANILLA EXTRACT
- 5 LARGE EGGS
- 390G | 3 CUPS ALL-PURPOSE FLOUR
- 1 TSP SALT
- 1 TSP BAKING POWDER
- 1/2 TSP BAKING SODA
- 160ML | 2/3 CUP FRESH ORANGE JUICE
- 60ML | 1/4 CUP TEQUILA
- 60ML | 1/4 CUP POMEGRANATE JUICE
- RED FOOD COLORING

FOR THE GLAZE:

- 100G | 1/2 CUP GRANULATED SUGAR
- 80ML | 1/3 CUP ORANGE JUICE
- 2 TBSP TEQUILA
- 60G | 1/2 CUP POWDERED SUGAR
- POMEGRANATE SEEDS FOR GARNISH

METHOD

STEP 1 PUT THE OVEN RACK TO THE LOWER THIRD LEVEL AND PREHEAT TO 175 C / 350 F. GREASE A 12 CUP / 25.5 CM BUNDT PAN AND DUST LIGHTLY WITH FLOUR THEN TAP OUT THE EXCESS.

STEP 2 BEAT THE BUTTER AND SUGAR TOGETHER FOR ABOUT 5 MINS UNTIL LIGHT AND FLUFFY. ADD THE ORANGE ZEST AND VANILLA AND BEAT IN, THEN BEAT THE EGGS IN ONE AT A TIME.

STEP 3 IN A NEW BOWL, WHISK TOGETHER THE FLOUR, SALT, BAKING POWDER, AND BAKING SODA TO COMBINE WELL. USE A LARGE METAL SPOON OR SPATULA TO GENTLY FOLD IN HALF OF THE FLOUR MIX INTO THE BUTTER MIX, THEN ADD THE ORANGE JUICE AND COMBINE WELL. FOLD IN THE REST OF THE FLOUR UNTIL EVERYTHING IS MOISTENED.

STEP 4 TRANSFER HALF OF THE BATTER TO A BOWL, THEN ADD POMEGRANATE JUICE AND A FEW DROPS OF RED FOOD COLORING. WHISK UNTIL WELL BLENDED, THEN ADD TEQUILA TO THE OTHER SET OF BATTER.

STEP 5 USING A SCOOP, DROP ALTERNATING COLORS OF BATTER INTO THE PAN, TAPPING TO REMOVE ANY AIR. BAKE FOR 45-55 MINS OR UNTIL A STICK COMES OUT DRY. COOL IN THE PAN FOR 20 MINS THEN MOVE TO A WIRE RACK TO COOL FULLY.

STEP 6 IN A SMALL SAUCEPAN, COMBINE AND HEAT THE SUGAR AND THE ORANGE JUICE TOGETHER ON A LOW HEAT, UNTIL DISSOLVED. REMOVE FROM THE HEAT AND STIR IN THE TEQUILA AND POWDERED SUGAR UNTIL ALL DISSOLVED. BRUSH THE GLAZE OVER THE SURFACE OF THE CAKE, SLICE AND SERVE WITH POMEGRANATE SEEDS. ENJOY!

MOCHA AMARETTO CREAM CAKE

PREP TIME: 30 MINS **COOK TIME:** 50 MINS **SERVES:** 10

ALMOND, CHOCOLATE AND COFFEE COME TOGETHER TO CREATE A RICH ITALIAN-INSPIRED CAKE NOT TO BE MISSED!

FOR THE PIE:

- 250G | 9 OZ SOFTENED UNSALTED BUTTER
- 125G | 4.5OZ CASTER SUGAR
- 125G | 4.5 OZ SOFT LIGHT BROWN SUGAR
- 3 EGGS
- 150G | 5.5 OZ ALL-PURPOSE FLOUR
- 1 TSP BAKING POWDER
- 30G | 1 OZ COCOA POWDER
- 100G | 3.5 OZ GROUND ALMONDS
- 5 TBSP INSTANT COFFEE
- 130G | 4.5 OZ DARK CHOCOLATE PLUS 30G 1 OZ TO DECORATE

FOR THE CREAM:

- 400ML | 14 OZ DOUBLE CREAM
- 3 TBSP AMARETTO

METHOD ♡

STEP 1 HEAT THE OVEN TO 180C / 360F AND LINE A 8-INCH SPRINGFORM CAKE TIN WITH BAKING PAPER. BEAT THE BUTTER AND ALL THE SUGAR TOGETHER WITH AN ELECTRIC WHISK UNTIL LIGHT AND FLUFFY. ADD THE EGGS ONE BY ONE, BEATING WELL TO MIX.

STEP 2 ADD AND LIGHTLY MIX IN THE FLOUR, BAKING POWDER, COCOA AND GROUND ALMONDS, THEN ADD THE COFFEE PASTE AND BEAT TOGETHER. MELT THE DARK CHOCOLATE AND STIR IN UNTIL JUST COMBINED.

STEP 3 POUR INTO THE CAKE TIN AND BAKE FOR 50 MINS UNTIL SLIGHTLY FUDGY IN THE MIDDLE, THEN ALLOW TO COOL COMPLETELY IN THE TIN. WHILST WAITING, GENTLY WHIP THE CREAM AND AMARETTO UNTIL IT STARTS TO THICKEN.

STEP 4 REMOVE FROM THE TIN AND PILE THE CREAM HIGH ON THE CAKE. CREATE CURLS BY DRAGGING A KNIFE ALONG THE DECORATING CHOCOLATE, SPRINKLE OVER, THEN SERVE AND ENJOY!

BOOZY WHITE CHOCOLATE PISTACHIO CRANBERRY COOKIES

PREP TIME: 30 MINS **COOK TIME:** 12 MINS **SERVES:** 22

WHISKEY INFUSED CRANBERRIES STEAL THE SHOW IN THESE DECADENT WHITE CHOCOLATE COOKIES.

FOR THE MIXTURE:

- 120ML | 1/2 CUP WHISKEY
- 200G | 1/2 CUP DRIED CRANBERRIES
- 125ML | 1/2 CUP UNSALTED BUTTER MELTED
- 65G | 1/3 CUP GRANULATED SUGAR
- 90G | 1/2 CUP LIGHT BROWN SUGAR PACKED
- 1 LARGE EGG
- 1 TSP VANILLA EXTRACT
- 1/2 TSP BAKING SODA
- 1/2 TSP SALT
- 180G | 1 1/2 CUPS ALL-PURPOSE FLOUR
- 200G | 1 CUP WHITE CHOCOLATE CHIPS
- 75G | 1/2 CUP PISTACHIOS SHELLED

METHOD ♡

STEP 1 IN A SAUCEPAN BRING THE WHISKEY TO A BOIL. THEN, IN A HEATPROOF BOWL, POUR THE WHISKEY OVER THE CRANBERRIES. ALLOW TO SOAK FOR AT LEAST 15 MINS, BUT EVEN LONGER TO MAKE STRONGER (EVEN OVERNIGHT!) DRAIN AND PAT DRY.

STEP 2 IN A LARGE BOWL MIX THE MELTED BUTTER, GRANULATED AND BROWN SUGAR UNTIL SMOOTH, THEN STIR IN THE EGG AND VANILLA EXTRACT. ADD THE BAKING SODA AND SALT, THEN MIX IN THE FLOUR SLOWLY UNTIL SMOOTH. ADD AND SLOWLY MIX IN THE WHITE CHOCOLATE, PISTACHIOS AND CRANBERRIES.

STEP 3 LINE A BAKING TRAY WITH PARCHMENT PAPER AND COVER WITH 2 TBSP SCOOPS OF THE MIXTURE. COVER WITH PLASTIC WRAP AND CHILL IN THE FRIDGE FOR AT LEAST 30 MINS.

STEP 4 PREHEAT THE OVEN TO 175C / 350 F AND SPREAD OUT THE COOKIES 2 INCHES APART ON THE TRAY. BAKE HALF OF THE COOKIES FOR 11-15 MINS, THEN REUSE THE PAPER AND BAKE THE REST. ALLOW EACH BATCH TO COOL FOR 10 MINS BEFORE REMOVING. SERVE AND ENJOY!

ESPRESSO MARTINI TIRAMISU

PREP TIME: 30 MINS SETTING TIME: 30 MINS SERVES: 12

EASY, INDULGENT AND SHOWSTOPPING. YOU'LL WANT TO MAKE THIS OVER AND OVER AGAIN.

FOR THE MIXTURE :

- 400ML | 14 OZ STRONG BLACK COFFEE (USE A CAFETIÈRE)
- 2 TSP BROWN SUGAR
- 4 TBSP VODKA
- 4 TBSP KAHLUA
- 500G | 18 OZ MASCARPONE
- 600ML | 21 OZ DOUBLE CREAM
- 3 TBSP ICING SUGAR
- 1 TBSP VANILLA EXTRACT
- 2 TBSP INSTANT ESPRESSO COFFEE POWDER
- 300G | 10.5 OZ SAVOIARDI SPONGE FINGERS
- 50G | 2 OZ DARK CHOCOLATE
- FOR DUSTING COCOA POWDER

METHOD

STEP 1 IN A SHALLOW BOWL, MIX THE COFFEE, BROWN SUGAR, VODKA, AND 3 TBSP OF KAHLÚA. IN A SEPARATE BOWL MIX THE MARSCAPONE FOR 2 MINS, THEN ADD IN THE DOUBLE CREAM, ICING SUGAR, AND VANILLA. BEAT IN WITH AN ELECTRIC BEATER UNTIL SOFT PEAKS FORM. PUT 1/3 OF THE KAHLÚA MIXTURE IN A NEW BOWL, THEN MIX IN THE COFFEE POWDER.

STEP 2 BRIEFLY DIP THE SPONGE FINGERS INTO THE VODKA AND COFFEE MIXTURE, THEN LAY IN THE BASE OF A LARGE SERVING DISH TO MAKE A SINGLE LAYER.

STEP 3 COVER THE SPONGES WITH 1/2 OF THE PLAIN CREAM, THEN GRATE OVER A LAYER OF DARK CHOCOLATE. LAY MORE SOAKED SPONGE FINGERS ON TOP, ADD A LAYER OF COFFEE CREAM AND THEN MORE CHOCOLATE. CREATE ANOTHER LAYER OF SPONGE, FINISH OFF WITH PLAIN CREAM AND MORE CHOCOLATE. CHILL FOR AT LEAST 4 HOURS, DUST WITH COCOA POWDER AND ENJOY!

BAILEYS NEW YORK CHEESECAKE

PREP TIME: 15 MINS **COOK TIME:** 45 MINS **SERVES:** 8

RICH AND BOOZY, THIS IS YOUR NEW FAVORITE CHEESECAKE.

FOR THE MIXTURE:

- 200G | 7 OZ STEM GINGER COOKIES, CRUSHED
- 45G | 1.6 OZ UNSALTED BUTTER, MELTED
- 600G | 21 OZ SOFT CHEESE
- 170ML | 5.7 OZ DOUBLE CREAM
- 150G | 5.3 OZ GOLDEN CASTER SUGAR
- 2 TBSP CORNFLOUR
- 5 TBSP BAILEYS ORIGINAL IRISH CREAM
- 3 EGGS
- 100G | 3.5 OZ WHITE CHOCOLATE, ROUGHLY CHOPPED

METHOD

STEP 1 PREHEAT THE OVEN TO 180 C / 355 F. MIX THE CRUSHED COOKIES AND BUTTER TOGETHER. TIP THE MIXTURE INTO A DEEP NON-STICK CAKE TIN, PRESSING DOWN WITH THE BACK OF A SPOON. ALLOW TO CHILL FOR 5 MINS.

STEP 2 USE AN ELECTRIC WHISK TO BEAT THE SOFT CHEESE, CREAM, SUGAR AND CORNFLOUR IN A LARGE BOWL UNTIL SMOOTH. WHISK IN THE BAILEYS AND EGGS UNTIL WELL COMBINED. POUR THE MIXTURE INTO THE TIN AND PLACE ON BAKING TRAY. SCATTER OVER THE WHITE CHOCOLATE, THEN COOK FOR 45 MINS OR UNTIL DARK GOLDEN.

STEP 3 WHEN READY, TURN OFF THE OVEN AND ALLOW THE CHEESECAKE TO COOL COMPLETELY WITH THE DOOR OPEN. CHILL IN THE FRIDGE OVERNIGHT, THEN SERVE WHEN READY. ENJOY!

CAKE

BAILEYS CAKE

PREP TIME: 40 MINS **COOK TIME:** 20 MINS **SERVES:** 12

THIS DECADENT THREE-TIERED DARK CHOCOLATE BAILEYS CAKE IS BEGGING TO BE SERVED AT CHRISTMAS!

FOR THE CAKE:

- 250G | 9 OZ BUTTER PLUS EXTRA
- 200G | 7 OZ SOFT LIGHT BROWN SUGAR
- 200G | 7 OZ DARK CHOCOLATE CUT INTO PIECES, PLUS EXTRA TO DECORATE
- 150ML | 5 OZ BAILEYS IRISH CREAM
- 250G | 9 OZ SELF-RAISING FLOUR
- 1 TSP BICARBONATE OF SODA
- 100G | 3.5 OZ COCOA POWDER
- 1/2 TSP FINE SEA SALT
- 4 LARGE EGGS
- 150G | 5 OZ YOGURT

FOR THE BUTTERCREAM:

- 250G | 9 OZ UNSALTED BUTTER SOFTENED
- 400G | 14 OZ POWDERED SUGAR
- 50ML | 1.75 OZ BAILEYS IRISH CREAM

METHOD ♡

STEP 1 PREHEAT THE OVEN TO 180 C / 360 F. GREASE THREE 8-INCH SPRINGFORM CAKE TINS. IN A SMALL PAN, GENTLY MELT THE BUTTER, SUGAR, AND DARK CHOCOLATE UNTIL COMBINED. POUR IN THE BAILEYS THEN LEAVE TO COOL FOR A BIT.

STEP 2 IN A LARGE BOWL, MIX THE FLOUR, BICARBONATE OF SODA, COCOA POWDER, AND SALT. POUR IN THE MELTED INGREDIENTS AND COMBINE. ADD THE EGGS, YOGURT, AND 50 ML / 1.75 OZ OF JUST BOILED WATER, THEN MIX WELL. DIVIDE THE MIXTURE BETWEEN THE THREE TINS AND BAKE FOR 20 MINS. LEAVE TO COOL FULLY.

STEP 3 MEANWHILE, BEAT THE BUTTER UNTIL LIGHT AND FLUFFY, THEN ADD THE POWDERED SUGAR A SPOONFUL AT A TIME, WHISKING WELL AFTER EACH. AFTER ALL THE SUGAR IS IN, BEAT FOR 2-3 MINS, THEN FOLD IN THE BAILEYS.

STEP 4 ON A CAKE STAND, SPREAD THE TOP OF ONE OF THE SPONGES WITH A THICK LAYER OF ICING. BUILD UP THE CAKE WITH A LAYER OF ICING BETWEEN EACH SPONGE, THEN COVER THE SIDES WITH THE REMAINING. GRATE OVER LOTS OF DARK CHOCOLATE, THEN SERVE AND ENJOY!

GRAPEFRUIT & ORANGE UPSIDE DOWN CAKE

PREP TIME: 45 MINS **COOK TIME:** 45 MINS **SERVES:** 8

RUBY RED WITH A GIN DRIZZLE, THIS CLASSY UPSIDE DOWN CAKE TICKS ALL THE BOXES.

FOR THE TOPPING:

- 2 TBSP SOFT LIGHT BROWN SUGAR
- 1 RUBY RED GRAPEFRUIT, CUT INTO 1/2 CM | 1/5 INCH SLICES
- 2 CLEMENTINES, CUT INTO 1/2 CM | 1/5 INCH SLICES
- TO SERVE: YOGURT OR CRÈME FRAÎCHE

FOR THE SPONGE:

- 250G | 8.8 OZ UNSALTED BUTTER, SOFTENED (PLUS EXTRA FOR THE TIN)
- 250G | 8.8 OZ SOFT LIGHT BROWN SUGAR
- 4 MEDIUM EGGS, BEATEN
- 150G | 5.3 OZ SELF-RAISING FLOUR
- 100G | 3.5 OZ GROUND ALMONDS
- 2 TSP ALMOND EXTRACT
- 1 TSP VANILLA EXTRACT
- ZEST OF 1 GRAPEFRUIT AND 1 CLEMENTINE

FOR THE DRIZZLE:

- JUICE OF 1 CLEMENTINE
- JUICE OF 1 GRAPEFRUIT
- 100ML | 3.4 OZ RUNNY HONEY
- 100ML | 3.4 FL OZ GIN (USE ONE WITH STRONG BOTANICALS)

METHOD

STEP 1 PREHEAT THE OVEN TO 180 C / 360 F. GREASE A 9-INCH SPRINGFORM CAKE TIN, THEN SPRINKLE THE BOTTOM WITH BROWN SUGAR. CAREFULLY ARRANGE THE SLICED FRUIT ON THE BOTTOM OF THE TIN, NOT LEAVING ANY GAPS.

STEP 2 WHISK THE BUTTER AND SUGAR IN A LARGE MIXING BOWL UNTIL LIGHT AND FLUFFY. ADD THE BEATEN EGGS IN ONE BY ONE, WHISKING EACH TIME.

STEP 3 FOLD IN THE FLOUR, GROUND ALMONDS, EXTRACTS, AND ZESTS USING A LARGE METAL SPOON. SPOON THE MIXTURE ON TOP OF THE FRUIT, SPREADING IT EVENLY ACROSS THE TIN. PUT THE CAKE TIN ON TOP OF A BAKING TRAY LINED WITH BAKING PAPER, THEN BAKE FOR 45-50 MINS. THE CAKE IS READY WHEN RISEN AND GOLDEN, OR A STICK COMES OUT CLEAN.

STEP 4 IN A SMALL PAN, SIMMER ALL OF THE DRIZZLE INGREDIENTS TOGETHER FOR 2-3 MINS, ALLOWING THE ALCOHOL TO BUBBLE OFF BUT KEEPING A HINT OF GIN FLAVORING.

STEP 5 CAREFULLY REMOVE THE CAKE TIN SIDES, THEN POUR 2-3 TSP OF THE DRIZZLE OVER THE SPONGE. USE A COOLING RACK TO CAREFULLY FLIP THE CAKE, THEN REDUCE THE DRIZZLE IN THE PAN FOR ANOTHER 3-4 MINS UNTIL SYRUPY AND THICK. ALLOW TO COOL FOR 5 MINS, THEN SPOON OVER THE FRUIT. SERVE WITH YOGURT OR CRÈME FRAÎCHE, THEN ENJOY!

MIMOSA BUTTER COOKIES

PREP TIME: 25 MINS **COOK TIME:** 15 MINS **SERVES:** 36

DELICIOUS ORANGEY COOKIES, PERFECT FOR SHARING WITH BIG GROUPS!

FOR THE MIXTURE :

- 240G | 1 CUP BUTTER SOFTENED
- 150G | 1 1/4 CUPS POWDERED SUGAR
- 2 TEASPOONS GRATED ORANGE ZEST
- 1 TEASPOON SALT
- 60ML | 1/4 CUP ORANGE JUICE
- 60ML | 1/4 CUP CHAMPAGNE
- 315G | 2 1/2 CUPS ALL-PURPOSE FLOUR

METHOD

STEP 1 PREHEAT THE OVEN TO 175 C / 350 F. CREAM THE BUTTER, POWDERED SUGAR, ORANGE ZEST, AND SALT IN A LARGE BOWL, UNTIL LIGHT AND FLUFFY. IN A JUG, MIX THE JUICE AND CHAMPAGNE. GRADUALLY ADD THE FLOUR TO THE CREAMED MIXTURE, ALTERNATING WITH THE JUICE MIXTURE. BEAT WELL EACH TIME.

STEP 2 CUT A SMALL HOLE INTO THE TIP OF A PASTRY BAG AND INSERT A 1M STAR TIP. FILL THE BAG WITH THE DOUGH AND PIPE 2-INCH CIRCLES ROUGHLY 2 INCHES APART ONTO A BAKING TRAY LINED WITH BAKING PAPER.

STEP 3 BAKE IN THE OVEN FOR 10-12 MINUTES, THEN ALLOW TO COOL FOR 5 MINS. MOVE TO WIRE RACKS TO COOL FURTHER, THEN SERVE AND ENJOY!

NEGRONI ORANGE CUPCAKES

PREP TIME: 30 MINS **COOK TIME:** 60 MINS **SERVES:** 12

WITH NOT ONE, NOT TWO, BUT THREE LIQUORS, THESE LUXURIOUS CUPCAKES PAY HOMAGE TO THE CLASSIC NEGRONI.

FOR THE CAKE:

- 150G | 5.3 OZ MARGARINE (SOFTENED)
- 150G | 5.3 OZ CASTER SUGAR
- 3 MEDIUM EGGS (BEATEN)
- 175G | 2.7 OZ PLAIN FLOUR
- 1 1/2 TSP BAKING POWDER
- 2 TBSP CAMPARI
- 2 TBSP SWEET VERMOUTH

FOR THE DRIZZLE:

- 2 TSP CAMPARI
- 2 TSP SWEET VERMOUTH
- JUICE OF 1 ORANGE
- 30G | 1 OZ CASTER SUGAR

FOR THE BUTTERCREAM:

- 150G | 5.3 OZ UNSALTED BUTTER (SOFTENED)
- 350G | 12.5 OZ POWDERED SUGAR
- 2 TBSP GIN
- 1 TSP ORANGE EXTRACT
- ZEST OF 1 ORANGE

FOR THE DECORATION:

- 1 ORANGE (SLICED)

METHOD

STEP 1 MAKE THE ORANGE SUGAR BY RUBBING THE GRANULATED SUGAR AND ORANGE ZEST WITH YOUR FINGERS UNTIL IT FEELS LIKE WET SAND AND THE COLOR IS EVEN.

STEP 2 PREHEAT THE OVEN TO 175 C TO 350 F, WITH A RACK IN BOTH THE UPPER AND LOWER THIRD. PREPARE TWO BAKING TRAYS WITH BAKING PAPER. IN A LARGE BOWL, BEAT TOGETHER THE BUTTER, EGG, SALT, BAKING SODA AND 300G / 1 1/2 CUPS OF ORANGE SUGAR, UNTIL LIGHT AND FLUFFY. ADD THE FLOUR AND THE COCOA POWDER AND MIX IN UNTIL JUST COMBINED. EVENLY SCOOP THE DOUGH INTO EVEN-SIZED BALLS (AROUND 2 1/2 TBSP). ROLL THE BALLS IN YOUR HANDS.

STEP 3 ROLL THE DOUGH BALLS IN THE ORANGE SUGAR, THEN PUT ON THE BAKING TRAYS AROUND 2 INCHES APART. GENTLY PRESS DOWN WITH YOUR PALM TO FLATTEN TO 3/4 INCH THICKNESS.

STEP 4 BAKE THE COOKIES FOR AROUND 12 MINS, SWAPPING THE TRAYS AROUND FROM TOP TO BOTTOM MIDWAY. LET COOL ON A WIRE RACK. MAKE THE ICING BY WHISKING THE INGREDIENTS TOGETHER UNTIL SMOOTH. DRIZZLE THE COOKIES WITH THE ICING, THEN GARNISH WITH SPARKLING SUGAR. ALLOW THE ICING TO SOLIDIFY, THEN SERVE AND ENJOY!

RUM AND RAISIN BUNDT CAKE

PREP TIME: 50 MINS **COOK TIME:** 50 MINS **SERVES:** 15

RUM AND RAISIN MAKES THE PERFECT COMBINATION - YOUR GUESTS WILL WANT SECONDS!

FOR THE CAKE

- 350G | 12.5 OZ RAISINS
- 100ML | 3.5 OZ DARK RUM
- 225G | 8 OZ BUTTER PLUS EXTRA FOR THE TIN
- 175G | 6 OZ LIGHT MUSCOVADO SUGAR
- 4 MEDIUM EGGS
- 350G | 12.5 OZ PLAIN FLOUR PLUS EXTRA FOR THE TIN
- 7G | 0.3 OZ SACHET FAST ACTION OR EASY BAKE YEAST
- 1 TBSP BAKING POWDER
- 2 TSP VANILLA EXTRACT
- 50ML | 1.75 OZ MILK

FOR THE FILLING:

- 100G | 3.5 OZ LIGHT MUSCOVADO SUGAR
- 50G | 2 OZ BUTTER
- 3 TBSP DARK RUM

METHOD ♡

STEP 1 THE NIGHT BEFORE, MIX THE RUM AND RAISINS AND ALLOW TO SOAK OVERNIGHT (STIR OCCASIONALLY IF YOU CAN, AND LEAVE FOR LONGER TO MAKE EVEN STRONGER).

STEP 2 THE DAY AFTER, DRAIN THE RAISINS BUT KEEP THE LEFTOVER RUM. PUT 200G / 7 OZ OF THE RAISINS IN A FOOD PROCESSOR ALONGSIDE THE RUM, BUTTER AND SUGAR, AND BLEND UNTIL VERY SMOOTH. ADD THE EGGS, FLOUR, YEAST, BAKING POWDER, VANILLA, MILK, AND A PINCH OF SALT AND BLEND AGAIN. TRANSFER TO A MIXING BOWL, COVER WITH PLASTIC WRAP AND LEAVE TO RISE FOR AN HOUR.

STEP 3 PREHEAT THE OVEN TO 170C / 355 F AND GREASE A LARGE BUNDT TIN, THEN LIGHTLY FLOUR, TAPPING AWAY THE EXCESS. FOLD THE REMAINING SOAKED RAISINGS THROUGH THE RISEN MIXTURE, THEN SPOON INTO THE TIN. SMOOTH THE TOP. BAKE FOR 50 MINS - 1HR, OR UNTIL A STICK COMES OUT CLEAN. LEAVE TO COOL ON A WIRE RACK.

STEP 4 ADD ALL OF THE GLAZE INGREDIENTS INTO A PAN AND HEAT UNTIL THE SUGAR HAS DISSOLVED, THEN ALLOW TO BUBBLE FURTHER UNTIL SHINY AND SAUCY. ALLOW TO COOL AND THICKEN SLIGHTLY, THEN POUR OVER THE CAKE. LEAVE TO COOL UNTIL SET, THEN SERVE AND ENJOY!

RASPBERRY MOSCOW MULE CAKE

PREP TIME: 20 MINS **COOK TIME:** 1 HR 15 MINS **SERVES:** 8

LIGHT AND FRESH, THIS CAKE COMBINES RASPBERRY, GINGER BEER, AND LIME TO MAKE AN IMPRESSIVE DESSERT!

FOR THE CAKE:

- 340G | 1 1/2 CUPS UNSALTED BUTTER, ROOM TEMPERATURE (3 STICKS)
- 550G | 2 3/4 CUPS
- GRANULATED SUGAR
- 5 LARGE EGGS
- 1 TBSP PURE VANILLA EXTRACT
- 1/2 TEASPOON KOSHER SALT
- 360G | 3 CUPS CAKE FLOUR, SIFTED
- 230G | 1 CUP CRABBIE'S
- SCOTTISH RASPBERRY GINGER BEER
- 1 PINT FRESH RASPBERRIES

FOR THE SYRUP:

- 120ML | 1/2 CUP CRABBIE'S SCOTTISH RASPBERRY GINGER BEER
- 100G | 1/2 CUP GRANULATED SUGAR
- FRESHLY SQUEEZED LIME JUICE FROM 2 LIMES

FOR THE FILLING:

- 170G | 1 1/2 CUPS POWDERED SUGAR
- FRESHLY SQUEEZED LIME JUICE FROM 2 LIMES
- 2 TSP GRATED LIME ZEST FROM 1 LIME

METHOD

STEP 1 PREHEAT THE OVEN TO 160 C / 315 F. GREASE A 6-CUP BUNDT PAN AND LIGHTLY FLOUR, TAPPING OUT THE EXCESS.

STEP 2 CREAM THE BUTTER AND SUGAR TOGETHER FOR AROUND 5-7 MINUTES, UNTIL IT'S PALE AND FLUFFY, THEN ADD THE EGGS IN ONE BY ONE. MIX INBETWEEN EACH. ADD IN THE VANILLA AND SALT AND MAKE SURE TO SCRAPE DOWN THE SIDES.

STEP 3 REDUCE THE SPEED AND ADD THE FLOUR ONE CUP AT A TIME. TAKING CARE NOT TO OVERMIX, THEN ADD IN THE GINGER BEER SLOWLY. SET MIX ASIDE.

STEP 4 COVER AND SMOOTH. BAKE FOR 75-80 MINS OR UNTIL A STICK COMES OUT CLEAN. LEAVE TO COOL FOR 10 MINS IN THE PAN, THEN TAKE OUT AND TRANSFER TO A PLATE.

STEP 5 TO MAKE THE SIMPLE SYRUP, HEAT THE GINGER BEER, SUGAR, AND LIME JUICE IN A SMALL SAUCEPAN OVER MEDIUM-HIGH HEAT. STIR, ALLOW TO COME TO A LIGHT BOIL, THEN REDUCE TO A SIMMER. SIMMER FOR ROUGHLY 5-7 MINUTES, UNTIL LIGHTLY REDUCED.

STEP 6 TO MAKE THE LIME GLAZE, STIR TOGETHER THE POWDERED SUGAR AND LIME JUICE, THEN STIR IN THE LIME ZEST ONCE COMBINED.

STEP 7 ONCE THE CAKE HAS COOLED, USE A FORK TO POKE ALL OVER. POUR THE SIMPLE SYRUP OVER THE CAKE THEN POUR OVER THE LIME GLAZE. SERVE AND ENJOY!

SANGRIA CAKE

PREP TIME: 45 MINS **COOK TIME:** 1 HR 20 MINS + 30 **SERVES:** 10

A SUMMERY CAKE PILED HIGH WITH FRUIT, AND SWIMMING IN A FRUITY RED WINE SAUCE.

FOR THE CAKE:

- 100G | 3.5 OZ PEARS, PEELED AND CHOPPED
- 100G | 3.5 OZ PEACHES OR NECTARINES, STONED AND CHOPPED
- 100G | 3.5 OZ STRAWBERRIES, HULLED AND CHOPPED
- 100G | 3.5 OZ CHERRIES, STONED AND CHOPPED
- 280G | 9.9 OZ GOLDEN CASTER SUGAR
- 225G | 7.9 OZ BUTTER, SOFTENED
- ZEST OF 1 ORANGE
- 150ML | 5 OZ RED WINE
- 225G | 7.9 OZ SELF-RAISING FLOUR
- 100G | 3.5 OZ GROUND ALMONDS
- 1 TSP BAKING POWDER
- 3 MEDIUM EGGS
- 50ML | 1.7 OZ ORANGE LIQUEUR (SUCH AS COINTREAU)
- 1 TBSP GRANULATED SUGAR

TO DECORATE:

- 1 SMALL ORANGE, CUT INTO WEDGES
- 1 LEMON, CUT INTO WEDGES
- A HANDFUL OF STRAWBERRIES (OPTIONAL)
- A HANDFUL OF CHERRIES (OPTIONAL)

METHOD ♡

STEP 1 MACERATE THE PEARS, PEACHES, STRAWBERRIES, AND CHERRIES IN A BOWL BY ADDING 2 OZ OF THE SUGAR AND MIXING. LEAVE FOR 30 MINS.

STEP 2 PREHEAT THE OVEN TO 160 C / 320 F, THEN GREASE AND LINE A ROUND LOOSE-BOTTOMED 9-INCH CAKE TIN.

STEP 3 IN LARGE BOWL ADD THE SUGAR, BUTTER, ORANGE ZEST, AND 100ML / 3.5OZ OF RED WINE, THEN WHISK UNTIL BLENDED. WHISK IN THE FLOUR, ALMONDS, BAKING POWDER, AND EGGS UNTIL SMOOTH. ADD HALF OF THE MACERATED FRUIT MIX, ALONG WITH 1 TBSP OF LIQUID FROM THE SAME BOWL, THEN GENTLY MIX WITH A SPOON. POUR THE MIX INTO THE TIN AND SMOOTH.

STEP 4 BAKE FOR 1HR - 1HR 15 MINS, UNTIL A STICK COMES OUT CLEAN. LEAVE IN THE TIN FOR 15 MINS TO COOL, THEN MOVE TO A WIRE RACK AND ALLOW TO COOL.

STEP 5 ONCE THE CAKE IS STILL A LITTLE WARM, POUR THE RED WINE, ORANGE LIQUEUR, AND GRANULATED SUGAR INTO A SAUCEPAN AND HEAT UNTIL MELTED. THEN BOIL THE LIQUID UNTIL SYRUPY. TURN THE CAKE OVER, PILE UP THE FRUIT ON TOP OF THE CAKE, THEN COVER IN THE SYRUP.

STEP 6 ADD THE DECORATIVE FRUIT, THEN SERVE. ENJOY!

KAHLÚA CHOCOLATE CHEESECAKE

PREP TIME: 35 MINS **COOK TIME:** 55 MINS **SERVES:** 10

A DELICIOUS CHOCOLATE AND COFFEE CHEESECAKE WITH A SPLASH OF BOOZE.

FOR THE PIE:

- 50G | 1.8 OZ BUTTER
- 225G | 8 OZ PLAIN CHOCOLATE DIGESTIVE BISCUIT CRUSHED

FOR THE FILLING:

- 225G | 8 OZ DARK CHOCOLATE (AT LEAST 50% COCOA SOLIDS), BROKEN
- 2 X 200G | 7 OZ FULL FAT SOFT CHEESE AT ROOM TEMPERATURE
- 100G | 3.5 OZ GOLDEN CASTER SUGAR
- 4 MEDIUM EGGS
- 284ML | 10 OZ CARTON DOUBLE CREAM
- 5 TBSP KAHLÚA

FOR THE TOPPING:

- 200ML | 7 OZ TUB CRÈME FRAÎCHE
- 2 TBSP KAHLÚA
- COCOA POWDER FOR DUSTING
- EXTRA KAHLÚA TO SERVE

METHOD

STEP 1 LIGHTLY GREASE A 9-INCH SPRING-FORM TIN. IN A LARGE SAUCEPAN, MELT THE BUTTER THEN STIR IN THE CRUSHED BISCUITS. PRESS THE MIXTURE INTO THE BAKING TIN WITH A SPOON, UNTIL LEVEL. CHILL WHILST MAKING THE FILLING.

STEP 2 OVER A PAN OF SIMMERING WATER, PLACE A HEAT-PROOF BOWL. PLACE THE CHOCOLATE INSIDE AND GENTLY MELT, STIRRING HALFWAY. WHEN MELTED, REMOVE THE BOWL. PREHEAT THE OVEN TO 160 C / 320 F.

STEP 3 IN A NEW LARGE BOWL, BEAT TOGETHER THE CHEESE AND SUGAR UNTIL FLUFFY. ADD THE EGGS ONE BY ONE, BEATING AFTER EACH ONE, TAKING CARE NOT TO OVERDO. SLOWLY BEAT IN THE MELTED CHOCOLATE, THEN THE CREAM AND KAHLÚA. POUR THIS MIXTURE ONTO THE BISCUIT BASE, THEN BAKE FOR 55 MINS. USE A BUTTER KNIFE TO LOOSEN THE CHEESECAKE FROM THE TIN. CHILL FOR AT LEAST 3 HOURS, OR OVERNIGHT.

STEP 4 TAKE THE CHEESECAKE OUT OF THE TIN. MAKE THE TOPPING BY COMBINING CRÈME FRAÎCHE AND KAHLÚA, AND SPREAD OVER THE CAKE. DUST WITH COCOA POWDER AND POUR A LITTLE BIT OF KAHLÚA OVER TO SERVE. ENJOY!

SPIKED BLACK FOREST CAKE

PREP TIME: 2 HRS **COOK TIME:** 45 MINS **SERVES:** 12

RICH AND DECADENT, TAKE A CHILDHOOD CLASSIC, ADD SOME BOOZE AND MAKE IT BOUJEE!

FOR THE CAKE:

- 250ML | 2 CUPS ALL-PURPOSE FLOUR
- 400G | 2 CUPS GRANULATED SUGAR
- 65G | 3/4 CUP COCOA POWDER SIFTED
- 2 TSP BAKING SODA
- 1 TSP BAKING POWDER
- 1 TSP SALT
- 110ML | 1/2 CUP VEGETABLE OIL
- 240G | 1 CUP BUTTERMILK ROOM TEMPERATURE
- 250G | 1 CUP HOT WATER OR HOT COFFEE
- 2 LARGE EGGS
- 2 TSP VANILLA EXTRACT

FOR THE SYRUP:

- 100G | 1/2 CUP GRANULATED SUGAR
- 125G | 1/2 CUP WATER
- 35G | 1/4 CUP CHERRY LIQUEUR

FOR THE DECORATION:

- 500G | 2 1/2 CUPS CHERRIES PITTED AND CUT IN HALF
- 1 BAR DARK CHOCOLATE FOR SHAVINGS (OPTIONAL)
- CHERRIES

FOR THE FROSTING:

- 715G | 3 CUP WHIPPING CREAM COLD
- 30G | 1/4 CUP POWDERED SUGAR SIFTED

FOR THE CHOCOLATE BARK:

- 250G | 9 OZ GOOD QUALITY DARK CHOCOLATE CHOPPED

METHOD ♡

STEP 1 PREHEAT THE OVEN TO 175 C / 350 F. GREASE TWO 8-INCH CAKE TINS, THEN LIGHTLY DUST WITH COCOA POWDER. LINE THE TINS WITH PARCHMENT.

STEP 2 MIX ALL OF THE DRY INGREDIENTS IN A BOWL USING A WHISK. THEN IN A DIFFERENT BOWL, MIX ALL THE WET INGREDIENTS TOGETHER, BUT MAKE SURE TO ADD THE HOT WATER GRADUALLY TO NOT COOK THE EGGS.

STEP 3 POUR THE WET INGREDIENTS INTO THE DRY INGREDIENTS AND MIX FOR A FEW MINUTES UNTIL COMBINED AND THE BATTER IS THIN.

STEP 4 SPLIT THE MIX BETWEEN THE TWO PANS AND BAKE FOR 45 MINS, OR UNTIL A STICK COMES OUT CLEAN. ALLOW TO COOL FOR 10 MINS THEN PUT ON A WIRE RACK TO COOL FULLY.

STEP 5 TO MAKE THE CHERRY LIQUEUR, MIX THE SUGAR AND WATER IN A SMALL SAUCEPAN AND BRING TO A BOIL. REDUCE THE HEAT AND SIMMER. ADD AND MIX IN THE CHERRY LIQUEUR AND LEAVE TO COOL.

STEP 6 TO MAKE THE WHIPPED CREAM FROSTING, WHIP THE INGREDIENTS TOGETHER UNTIL THEY FORM STIFF PEAKS.

STEP 7 FOR THE CHOCOLATE BAR, MELT THE CHOCOLATE IN A HEAT-SAFE BOWL OVER A PAN OF BOILING WATER, OR IN 20 SECOND INTERVALS IN THE MICROWAVE. THEN SPREAD THE MELTED CHOCOLATE IN A THIN LAYER ON A LARGE SHEET OF BAKING PAPER. ROLL UP THE PAPER FROM THE SHORT SIDE, PLACE ON A BAKING TRAY AND PUT IN THE FRIDGE OR FREEZER UNTIL SOLID. WHEN READY, UNROLL THE PAPER TO CREATE YOUR BARK.

STEP 8 CUT YOUR CAKE SPONGES IN HALF HORIZONTALLY, THEN BRUSH ONE WITH THE CHERRY LIQUEUR AND PLACE ON A CAKE STAND. COVER WITH A CUP OF WHIPPED CREAM AND SPREAD OVER, THEN TOP WITH A CUP OF CHERRIES AND PRESS IN. REPEAT OVER WITH EACH LAYER, THEN COVER THE OUTSIDE OF THE CAKE WITH FROSTING. DECORATE YOUR CAKE WITH THE CHOCOLATE BARK SHAVINGS, AND CHERRIES THEN SERVE AND ENJOY!

CHOCOLATE CHIPS COOKIES WITH TENNESSEE WHISKEY

PREP TIME: 30 MINS **COOK TIME:** 10 MINS **SERVES:** 36

THESE WHISKEY COOKIES WOULD BE PERFECT FOR SANTA ON CHRISTMAS EVE – OR FOR YOU FOR ANY OCCASION!

FOR THE MIXTURE :

- 313G | 2 1/2 CUPS ALL-PURPOSE FLOUR
- 1 TEASPOON BAKING SODA
- 1 TEASPOON SALT
- 227G | 1 CUP BUTTER, SOFTENED
- 200G | 1 CUP WHITE SUGAR
- 220G | 1 CUP FIRMLY PACKED BROWN SUGAR
- 2 EGGS, BEATEN
- 1 TABLESPOON TENNESSEE WHISKEY
- 1 TEASPOON VANILLA EXTRACT
- 1 (340G | 12 OZ) BAG SEMI-SWEET CHOCOLATE CHIPS

METHOD

STEP 1 PREHEAT THE OVEN TO 175 C / 350 F. IN A BOWL, SIFT TOGETHER THE FLOUR, BAKING SODA, AND SALT.

STEP 2 IN A LARGE BOWL USE AN ELECTRIC WHISK TO BEAT TOGETHER THE BUTTER, WHITE SUGAR, AND BROWN SUGAR. ADD THE EGGS ONE AFTER THE OTHER, BEATING WELL INBETWEEN. MIX IN THE WHISKEY AND VANILLA EXTRACT UNTIL COMBINED.

STEP 3 ADD THE FLOUR MIXTURE AND COMBINE UNTIL JUST MIXED IN, THEN GENTLY FOLD IN THE CHOCOLATE CHIPS. ROLL THE DOUGH INTO 1-INCH BALLS AND ARRANGE ON A BAKING SHEET 2 INCHES APART.

STEP 4 BAKE IN THE OVEN FOR 9-12 MINUTES UNTIL THE EDGES ARE LIGHTLY BROWNED. ALLOW TO COOL ON A WIRE RACK, THEN SERVE AND ENJOY!

CHOCOLATE GUINNESS CAKE

PREP TIME: 20 MINS COOK TIME: 1 HR SERVES: 10

A MATCH MADE IN HEAVEN, THIS CHOCOLATE GUINNESS CAKE IS A MUST-BAKE.

FOR THE CAKE:

- 250ML | 9 OZ GUINNESS
- 175G | 6 OZ SALTED BUTTER CUBED, PLUS EXTRA FOR THE TIN
- 75G | 3 OZ DARK CHOCOLATE ROUGHLY CHOPPED
- 1 TBSP VANILLA BEAN PASTE
- 3 LARGE EGGS
- 100G | 3.5 OZ SOURED CREAM
- 200G | 7 OZ CASTER SUGAR
- 75G | 3 OZ SOFT DARK BROWN SUGAR
- 300G | 10.5 OZ PLAIN FLOUR
- 2 TSP BICARBONATE OF SOBA
- 40G | 1.5 OZ COCOA POWDER

FOR THE ICING:

- 300ML | 10.5 OZ DOUBLE CREAM
- 50G | 2 OZ SOFT DARK BROWN SUGAR
- 3 TBSP COCOA POWDER

METHOD

STEP 1 PREHEAT THE OVEN TO 180 C / 360 F AND GREASE A LOOSE-BOTTOMED 9-INCH CAKE TIN, THEN LINE WITH PARCHMENT PAPER.

STEP 2 IN A MEDIUM PAN, ADD THE GUINNESS, BUTTER, CHOCOLATE, AND VANILLA TOGETHER, THEN GENTLY HEAT AND COMBINE UNTIL SMOOTH. ALLOW TO COOL FOR 5 MINS.

STEP 3 ONCE IT HAS COOLED SLIGHTLY, ADD THE EGGS AND WHISK. THEN ADD THE SOURED CREAM AND WHISK UNTIL SMOOTH. ADD THE REST OF THE DRY INGREDIENTS TOGETHER IN A LARGE BOWL AND MIX. THEN SLOWLY ADD THE WET INGREDIENTS, WHISKING TOGETHER UNTIL THE BATTER IS SMOOTH.

STEP 4 TRANSFER THE BATTER TO THE PREPARED TIN AND BAKE FOR 1HR - 1HR 15 MINS, UNTIL A STICK COMES OUT CLEAN. ALLOW TO COOL COMPLETELY.

STEP 5 FOR THE ICING, WHISK ALL OF THE INGREDIENTS TOGETHER UNTIL SOFT PEAKS FORM. DOLLOP THE ICING ON TOP OF THE CAKE ONCE OUT OF THE TIN, SPREAD IT AROUND AND THEN GET READY TO SERVE. ENJOY!

BRANDY PUDDING

PREP TIME: 45 MINS **COOK TIME:** 3 HRS **SERVES:** 8

IMPRESSIVE AND PERFECTLY CHRISTMASSY, SERVE THIS UP ON THE BIG DAY INSTEAD!

FOR THE PUDDING:

- 250G | 8.8 OZ BLOCK STONED DATES, FINELY CHOPPED
- 125G | 4.4 OZ BUTTER, SOFTENED (PLUS EXTRA FOR GREASING)
- 85G | 3 OZ LIGHT MUSCOVADO SUGAR
- 140G | 4.9 OZ SELF-RAISING FLOUR
- 1 TSP BAKING POWDER
- 2 LARGE EGGS
- 50G | 1.8 OZ RAISINS
- 50G | 1.8 OZ CHOPPED CANDIED PEEL
- 50G | 1.8 OZ DARK GLACÉ CHERRIES, HALVED
- 50G | 1.8 OZ PECANS, CHOPPED
- 50G | 1.8 OZ STEM GINGER, CHOPPED

FOR THE SYRUP:

- 100G | 3.5 OZ CASTER SUGAR
- 100ML | 3.4 OZ BRANDY

TO SERVE:

- BUTTERSCOTCH SAUCE
- 1 HOLLY SPRIG, TO GARNISH

METHOD

STEP 1 PREHEAT THE OVEN TO 180 C / 360 F. SOAK THE DATES IN A BOWL OF 250ML / 8 OZ OF BOILING WATER AND LEAVE. GREASE A PUDDING BASIN AND PUT IN A DISC OF BAKING PAPER.

STEP 2 IN A LARGE BOWL BEAT TOGETHER BUTTER, SUGAR, FLOUR, BAKING POWDER, AND EGGS. ADD THE DATE MIX (INCLUDING WATER) ONCE COOLED, AND MIX. THE BATTER WILL BE RUNNY.

STEP 3 MIX IN THE FRUITS, PECANS, AND GINGER, THEN POUR THE MIXTURE INTO THE PUDDING BASIN, THEN COVER WITH PLEATED PARCHMENT PAPER AND FOIL. FILL A ROASTING TIN HALFWAY WITH BOILING WATER AND PUT THE BASIN IN. STEAM THE PUDDING IN THE OVEN FOR 3 HOURS.

STEP 4 TO MAKE THE BRANDY SYRUP, MIX THE SUGAR WTH 75ML / 2.5 OZ OF WATER AND HEAT IN A PAN UNTIL SYRUPY. ADD THE BRANDY, MIX, THEN SET ASIDE. WHEN THE PUDDING IS OUT OF THE OVEN, POUR THE BRANDY OVER TO SOAK IN. STORE IN THE FRIDGE UNTIL READY TO SERVE.

STEP 5 TO SERVE, HEAT IN THE OVEN OR MICROWAVE, THEN TURN OUT ON A PLATE. SERVE WITH BUTTERSCOTCH SAUCE AND A SPRIG OF HOLLY FOR THE CHRISTMAS SPIRIT!

PIÑA COLADA UPSIDE DOWN CAKE

PREP TIME: 1HR 30 MINS **COOK TIME:** 45 MINS **SERVES:** 8

TROPICAL AND SYRUPY, THIS UPSIDE DOWN CAKE WILL LIVEN UP ANY SUMMER BBQ!

FOR THE CAKE:

- 226G | 8 OZ SELF RAISING FLOUR
- 226G | 8 OZ BUTTER
- 226G | 8 OZ CASTER SUGAR
- 4 EGGS
- 1 TSP VANILLA ESSENCE
- 1 LARGE TIN OF PINEAPPLE RINGS IN SYRUP OR JUICE
- GLACE CHERRY HALVES

FOR THE SYRUP:

- 4 TBSP PIÑA COLADA SYRUP
- 2 TBSP RUM
- 2 TBSP GOLDEN SYRUP

METHOD ♡

STEP 1 PREHEAT THE OVEN TO 180 C / 360 F, THEN GREASE YOUR CAKE DISH AND LINE WITH PARCHMENT PAPER.

STEP 2 MAKE THE SYRUP BY MIXING THE PINA COLADA SYRUP, RUM AND GOLDEN SYRUP IN A BOWL.

STEP 3 IN A LARGE BOWL, MIX THE BUTTER AND SUGAR TOGETHER UNTIL LIGHT AND FLUFFY, THEN ADD THE EGGS ONE BY ONE, BEATING WELL EACH TIME. SIFT IN THE FLOUR AND GENTLY FOLD IN. ADD THE VANILLA ESSENCE AND MIX.

STEP 4 IN A LARGE BOWL, POUR IN THE SYRUP AND PLACE THE DRAINED PINEAPPLE RINGS IN. COVER THE BOTTOM THE OF THE CAKE TIN WITH SPOONFULS OF SYRUP. MOVE THE RINGS FROM THE SYRUP BOWL TO THE CAKE TIN, TO COVER THE BASE. CUT THEM WHERE NEEDED. PLACE THE CHERRIES INTO THE PINEAPPLE RINGS AND SPOON MORE SYRUP OVER. POUR IN THE CAKE BATTER.

STEP 5 COOK FOR 45 MINS - 1 HR, UNTIL A STICK COMES OUT CLEAN. LEAVE TO COOL. POKE SOME HOLES IN THE CAKE WITH A FORK, AND COVER WITH THE REST OF THE SYRUP. ALLOW TO SINK IN EACH TIME BEFORE ADDING MORE.

STEP 6 TURN THE CAKE UPSIDE DOWN ONTO A PLATE SO THE PINEAPPLES ARE ON TOP. SERVE AND ENJOY!

STRAWBERRY PINK CHAMPAGNE CUPCAKES

PREP TIME: 15 MINS **COOK TIME:** 20 MINS **SERVES:** 24

PINK, FRUITY, AND SWEET, THESE CUPCAKES ARE THE PERFECT VALENTINE'S TREAT!

FOR THE CUPCAKES:

- 375G | 3 CUPS ALL PURPOSE FLOUR
- 3 TSP BAKING POWDER
- 1/2 TSP SALT
- 400G | 2 CUPS SUGAR
- 2 STICKS UNSALTED BUTTER, SOFTENED
- 6 LARGE EGG WHITES
- 240ML | 1 CUP FRESH STRAWBERRIES, PUREED
- 240ML | 1 CUP PINK CHAMPAGNE

FOR THE FROSTING:

- 2 STICKS UNSALTED BUTTER, SOFTENED
- 450G | 1 LB POWDERED SUGAR
- 3 TBSP PINK CHAMPAGNE
- 3 TBSP FRESH STRAWBERRIES, PURÉED

METHOD ♡

STEP 1 PREHEAT THE OVEN TO 175 C / 350 F. LINE A CUPCAKE TRAY WITH 24 CUPCAKE CASES. WHISK TOGETHER THE STRAWBERRY PURÉE AND CHAMPAGNE IN A BOWL.

STEP 2 IN A LARGE BOWL, WHISK THE FLOUR, BAKING POWDER, AND SALT. IN A DIFFERENT BOWL, BEAT THE UNSALTED BUTTER AND SUGAR TOGETHER UNTIL LIGHT AND FLUFFY. GRADUALLY ADD THE EGG WHITES, BEATING WELL EACH TIME.

STEP 3 ADD HALF OF THE FLOUR MIXTURE, BEATING WELL UNTIL COMBINED, THEN ADD THE CHAMPAGNE MIXTURE. AFTER BEATING WELL, ADD THE REST OF THE FLOUR, AND COMBINE, INCLUDING THE MIX ON THE SIDES. POUR THE BATTER INTO THE LINED CUPCAKE TINS EVENLY.

STEP 4 BAKE FOR 17-18 MINUTES UNTIL A STICK COMES OUT CLEAN. LET COOL ON A WIRE RACK.

STEP 5 FOR THE ICING, BEAT THE BUTTER UNTIL LIGHT AND FLUFFY, THEN ADD THE REST OF THE INGREDIENTS. INITIALLY MIX AT A LOW SPEED, THEN CHANGE TO HIGH ONCE COMBINED. COVER THE CUPCAKES WITH THE ICING AND ENJOY!

BAILEYS CHOCOLATE TIFFIN

PREP TIME: 30 MINS **COOK TIME:** 10 MINS **SERVES:** 36

FILLED WITH THREE KINDS OF CHOCOLATE AND A HEALTHY HELPING OF BAILEYS LIQUEUR, THERE'S NOTHING NOT TO LOVE ABOUT THIS TIFFIN.

FOR THE MIXTURE :

- 100G | 3.5 OZ RAISINS OR SULTANAS
- 6 TBSP BAILEYS OR ANOTHER IRISH CREAM
- 250G | 9 OZ 72% DARK CHOCOLATE CHOPPED INTO SMALL PIECES
- 250G | 9 OZ MILK CHOCOLATE CHOPPED INTO SMALL PIECES
- 100G | 3.5 OZ UNSALTED BUTTER
- 300G | 10.5 OZ SHORTBREAD CRUMBLED INTO CHUNKS
- 225G | 8 OZ JAR MARASCHINO CHERRIES DRAINED AND HALVED
- 200G | 7 OZ WHITE CHOCOLATE
- TO SPRINKLE EDIBLE GOLD GLITTER

METHOD ♡

STEP 1 LINE AN 8-INCH TIN WITH BAKING PAPER. MICROWAVE THE RAISINS AND 2 TBSPS OF BAILEYS IN A SAFE BOWL COVERED WITH PLASTIC WRAP. LEAVE COVERED TO ALLOW TO SOAK.

STEP 2 MELT HALF OF THE DARK AND MILK CHOCOLATE IN A PAN WITH BUTTER UNTIL COMPLETELY SMOOTH, THEN ADD THE RAISINS, THE REST OF THE BAILEYS, THE SHORTBREAD PIECES, AND THE CHERRIES. POUR INTO THE TIN AND SMOOTH.

STEP 3 ALLOW TO CHILL IN THE FRIDGE FOR AN HOUR.

STEP 4 MELT THE LEFTOVER DARK, WHITE, AND MILK CHOCOLATE IN SEPARATE BOWLS / PANS. BLOB THEM ONTO THE TOP OF THE TIFFIN, THEN SWIRL AROUND TO MAKE PATTERNS.

STEP 5 PUT THE TIFFIN BACK IN THE FRIDGE FOR ANOTHER 4 HOURS, BUT SERVE AT ROOM TEMPERATURE. ENJOY!

RUM & COCONUT TREACLE TART

PREP TIME: 30 MINS **COOK TIME:** 30 MINS **SERVES:** 8

A DELICIOUS SYRUPY TART WTH A RUM TWIST, BRING THE TASTE OF THE CARIBBEAN TO YOUR DESSERT!

FOR THE TREACLE TART:

- 200G | 7 OZ BOUGHT SHORTCRUST PASTRY
- 85G | 3 OZ BLACK TREACLE
- 175G | 6 OZ GOLDEN SYRUP
- FINELY GRATED ZEST AND JUICE OF 1 LIME
- 4 TBSP | 2 OZ DARK RUM
- 50G | 2 OZ FRESH BROWN BREADCRUMBS
- 85G | 3 OZ SWEETENED, TENDERISED COCONUT

FOR THE RUM CREAM:

- 3 TBSP DARK RUM
- 284ML | 9.6 OZ CARTON DOUBLE CREAM
- 3 TBSP POWDERED SUGAR

METHOD

STEP 1 PREHEAT THE OVEN TO 190 C / 375 F. LINE A 9-INCH SHALLOW DISH WITH THE PASTRY ROLLED OUT TO 1/8 INCH THICK, LEAVING THE EXTRA HANGING OVER THE SIDES. POKE THE BASE WITH A FORK A FEW TIMES AND CHILL FOR A MINIMUM OF 30 MINS.

STEP 2 MIX TOGETHER THE TREACLE'S WET INGREDIENTS IN A LARGE BOWL, THEN STIR IN THE BREADCRUMBS AND COCONUT. PUT THE PASTRY DISH ON TOP OF A BAKING TRAY, THEN POUR THE SYRUP FILLING OVER THE BASE. BAKE FOR 15 MINS, REDUCE THE HEAT TO 160 C / 320 F, THEN BAKE FOR ANOTHER 15 MINS. THE PASTRY SHOULD BE BROWNING.

STEP 3 FOR THE RUM CREAM, WHISK ALL OF THE INGREDIENTS TOGETHER UNTIL SOFT PEAKS FORM. CHILL UNTIL NEEDED. ALLOW THE TART TO COOL SLIGHTLY THEN TRIM THE EDGES, AND SERVE WITH THE RUM CREAM. ENJOY!

MULLED WINE WINTER PUDDINGS

PREP TIME: 45 MINS + CHILLING AND INFUSING OVERNIGHT **SERVES:** 6

THE TASTE OF CHRISTMAS, THESE PUDDINGS ARE FULL OF DELICIOUS FRUIT - AND MULLED WINE!

FOR THE MIXTURE :

- 600G | 21 OZ FROZEN BLACK FOREST FRUITS DEFROSTED
- 75G | 3 OZ CASTER SUGAR
- 1/2 LEMON JUICED
- 200ML | 7 OZ FRUITY RED WINE
- 1 STAR ANISE
- 1 CINNAMON STICK
- 2 CLOVES
- 2 STRIPS ORANGE PEEL
- 10 SLICES WHITE BREAD

METHOD

STEP 1 COOK THE FRUIT, SUGAR, AND LEMON JUICE IN A PAN ON MEDIUM HEAT, FOR 5 MINS. SIEVE OVER A BOWL UNTIL ALL THE JUICE HAS DRAINED.

STEP 2 SIMMER THE FRUIT SYRUP WITH THE WINE, SPICES, AND ORANGE PEEL TOGETHER FOR 5 MINS, THEN SET ASIDE FOR AN HOUR TO INFUSE.

STEP 3 LINE 6 SMALL PUDDING MOLDS WITH PLASTIC WRAP, LEAVING ENOUGH TO COVER FULLY AFTER. CUT SIX 2-INCH CIRCLE DISCS FROM 2 OF THE PIECES OF BREAD. THEN USE THE REST OF THE BREAD TO CUT OUT SIX 3-INCH DISCS FOR THE LIDS, THEN 1.5 X 2-INCH RECTANGLES WITH THE REST OF THE BREAD. DIP THE SMALLEST CIRCLES IN THE SYRUP THEN PUT IN THE BASE OF THE MOLDS. THEN DIP THE RECTANGLES AND FIT THEM AROUND THE EDGES OF THE MOLDS, OVERLAPPING AND STICKING TOGETHER. FILL UP THE PUDDINGS WITH THE FRUIT, AND ADD A TBSP OF SYRUP. SOAK THE LARGEST CIRCLES, TOP THE PUDDINGS, THEN COVER WITH THE REMAINING PLASTIC WRAP.

STEP 4 PUT THE PUDDINGS ON A BAKING TRAY, THEN PUT ANOTHER TRAY ON TOP WITH A WEIGHT. LEAVE TO CHILL FOR 6 OR SO HOURS, OR OVERNIGHT.

STEP 5 UNWRAP THE MOLDS WHEN READY AND TURN OUT THE PUDDINGS ONTO PLATES. SERVE WITH THE LEFTOVER SYRUP, ENJOY!

BOURBON BALLS

PREP TIME: 10 MINS **COOK TIME:** 2 MINS + A WEEK CHILLING
SERVES: 24

DELICIOUS BITE-SIZED BOOZY CHOCOLATE BALLS!

FOR THE MIXTURE :

- 170G | 6 OZ SEMI-SWEET CHOCOLATE CHIPS
- 100G | 3.5 OZ WHITE SUGAR
- 3 TBSP CORN SYRUP
- 120ML | 4 FL OZ RUM
- 300G | 10.6 OZ CRUSHED VANILLA WAFERS
- 120G | 4.2 OZ CHOPPED WALNUTS (OPTIONAL)
- 40G | 1.4 OZ POWDERED SUGAR

METHOD

STEP 1 MELT THE CHOCOLATE CHIPS IN A MICROWAVE-SAFE BOWL, HEATING FOR 1 MINS, STIRRING, THEN HEATING FOR 20 SECONDS EACH, STIRRING EACH TIME UNTIL MELTED AND SMOOTH.

STEP 2 ADD THE SUGAR AND CORN SYRUP, THEN STIR. MIX IN THE RUM, THEN ADD THE CRUSHED VANILLA WAFERS AND CHOPPED NUTS. MIX WELL, THEN COVER AND PUT IN THE FRIDGE UNTIL FIRM.

STEP 3 ROLL THE MIXTURE INTO LITTLE BALLS, THEN ROLL IN A MIX OF GROUND NUTS AND POWDERED SUGAR.

STEP 4 STORE FOR A WEEK IN A COVERED CONTAINER TO ALLOW THE FLAVORS TO BLEND, THEN SERVE AND ENJOY!

BEER CUPCAKES WITH SALTED CARAMEL DRIZZLE

PREP TIME: 25 MINS **COOK TIME:** 1 HR 5 MINS **SERVES:** 12

BEER AND SALT - THERE'S NEVER BEEN A BETTER COMBINATION. SO BRING THEM TOGETHER ALONGSIDE CARAMEL IN DELICIOUS CUPCAKES!

FOR THE CUPCAKES:

- 188G | 6.6 OZ FLOUR
- 133G | 4.7 OZ SUGAR
- 120ML | 4 OZ CRAFT BEER
- 120ML | 4 OZ MELTED BUTTER
- 1 EGG
- 1 TSP BAKING SODA
- 1 TSP SALT
- 1 TSP VANILLA EXTRACT

FOR THE SALTED CARAMEL:

- 200G | 7 OZ GRANULATED SUGAR
- 85G | 3 OZ UNSALTED BUTTER
- 120ML | 4 OZ HEAVY CREAM
- 1 TSP SALT

METHOD ♡

STEP 1 COMBINE YOUR MELTED BUTTER AND SUGAR IN A LARGE MIXING BOWL, ONCE MIXED ADD THE EGG AND MIX AGAIN. NOW ADD YOUR VANILLA AND BEER.

STEP 2 COMBINE YOUR DRY INGREDIENTS TOGETHER IN A SEPARATE BOWL AND ADD VERY GRADUALLY TO YOUR WET MIXTURE, BEING CAREFUL NOT TO OVER STIR.

STEP 3 ADD YOUR MIXTURE TO THE CUPCAKE LINERS AND PLACE IN A PREHEATED OVEN AT 175 C / 350 F AND BAKE FOR 18 MINUTES.

STEP 4 TO MAKE YOUR SALTED CARAMEL, IN A HEAVY DUTY SAUCEPAN HEAT YOUR SUGAR OVER A MEDIUM HEAT STIRRING CONSTANTLY. AFTER 6 MINUTES THE SUGAR SHOULD HAVE TURNED BROWN AND FORMED CLUMPS BEFORE MELTING. ONCE MELTED ADD IN YOUR BUTTER, ENSURING TO WHISK VIGOROUSLY.

STEP 5 VERY SLOWLY POUR YOUR CREAM INTO THE SUGAR AND BUTTER MIXTURE AGAIN STIRRING CONSTANTLY, ALLOW THIS TO SIT ON THE HEAT FOR ANOTHER MINUTE BEFORE REMOVING AND STIRRING IN THE SALT.

STEP 6 ALLOW YOUR SALTED CARAMEL TO THICKEN WHILE IT COOLS BEFORE USING TO DRIZZLE ON TOP OF YOUR CUPCAKES. THE REST OF YOUR CARAMEL CAN BE STORED FOR UP TO A MONTH IN THE FRIDGE IF SEALED TIGHTLY.

BAILEYS IRISH CREAM SCONES

PREP TIME: 15 MINS **COOK TIME:** 15 MINS **SERVES:** 8

BOOZY SCONES WILL MAKE ANY AFTERNOON TEA BETTER!

FOR THE MIXTURE :

- 304G | 2 1/8 CUPS ALL PURPOSE FLOUR
- 6 TBSPS SUGAR
- 1 TSP BAKING POWDER
- 1/2 TSP SALT
- 113G | 1 STICK UNSALTED BUTTER, COLD AND CUBED
- 1 TSP INSTANT ESPRESSO POWDER
- 60ML | 1/4 CUP BAILEY'S IRISH CREAM
- 177ML | 3/4 CUP HEAVY CREAM
- 113G | 1/2 CUP SEMI-SWEET OR DARK CHOCOLATE, CHOPPED OR CHOCOLATE CHIPS

METHOD

STEP 1 PREHEAT TO 205 C / 400 F AND KEEP THE BAKING TRAY IN THE OVEN. CUT THE BUTTER INTO PEA-SIZED PIECES AND PLACE IN THE FREEZER.

STEP 2 HEAT THE BAILEY'S FOR 30 SECONDS IN THE MICROWAVE, THEN ADD 1 TSP OF ESPRESSO POWDER AND COMBINE UNTIL SMOOTH. COOL IN THE FRIDGE. IN A LARGE BOWL COMBINE THE FLOUR, SUGAR, BAKING POWDER, AND SALT, AND MIX.

STEP 3 ADD THE CHOPPED UP BUTTER INTO THE FLOUR AND USE YOUR HANDS OR FORKS TO MIX IN THE BUTTER UNTIL IT BECOMES SAND-LIKE.

STEP 4 CREATE A WELL IN THE FLOUR AND BUTTER MIX, THEN POUR IN THE BAILEYS AND ALL BUT A QUARTER OF THE HEAVY CREAM. MIX WITH YOUR HAND UNTIL ALL IS WET AND THE DOUGH STICKS TOGETHER. ADD THE REST OF THE CREAM BY HALF A TBSP A TIME IF IT IS TOO CRUMBLY.

STEP 5 ADD IN THE CHOCOLATE CHIPS AND FOLD IN. FLOUR A SURFACE THEN TURN OUT THE DOUGH, THEN SHAPE IT INTO A 1-INCH THICK CIRCLE. CUT THE DOUGH INTO 8 TRIANGLES, PUT ON BAKING PAPER 2 INCHES APART AND MOVE TO THE HOT TRAY. BAKE FOR 13-18 MINS UNTIL GOLDEN BROWN. SERVE AND ENJOY!

RUM TARTE TATIN

PREP TIME: 45 MINS **COOK TIME:** 30 MINS **SERVES:** 6

THIS TARTE IS SURE TO IMPRESS AND WILL BE HIT FOR LOVERS OF APPLE AND RUM!

FOR THE MIXTURE :

- 60G | 2 OZ GOLDEN CASTER SUGAR
- 40G | 1.5 OZ SOFT LIGHT BROWN SUGAR
- 50G | 1.8 OZ BUTTER
- 50ML | 1.8 OZ DARK RUM
- 4 RUSSET APPLES (OR OTHER EATING APPLE) PEELED, CORED AND HALVED
- 150G | 5 OZ READY-MADE PUFF PASTRY

METHOD

STEP 1 PREHEAT THE OVEN TO 180 C / 360 F. PUT THE SUGARS IN AN OVENPROOF FRYING PAN, AND HEAT OVER A MEDIUM HEAT. WHEN IT HAS BECOME GOLDEN CARAMEL, TAKE OFF THE HEAT THEN STIR IN THE BUTTER AND RUM. MAKE SURE TO MIX QUICKLY UNTIL WELL COMBINED.

STEP 2 ON A LOWER HEAT, COOK THE APPLES IN THE CARAMEL MIXTURE FOR 5 MINS OR UNTIL SLIGHTLY SOFTENED. PLACE THEM CURVED-SIDE DOWN IN THE PAN. TAKE OFF THE HEAT.

STEP 3 USE A ROUGHLY 9-INCH PLATE TO CUT A CIRCLE OUT OF THE PASTRY, THE PLACE IT ON TOP OF THE APPLES, TUCKING AROUND THE EDGES. PUT THE PAN IN THE OVEN FOR 25-30 MINS, ALLOW TO COOL FOR 5 MINS, THEN TURN OUT ONTO A PLATE. SERVE AND ENJOY!

CHOCOLATE RED WINE CAKE

PREP TIME: 25 MINS **COOK TIME:** 45 MINS **SERVES:** 12

A FLUFFY AND RICH PUDDING WITH A PERFECTLY BOOZY FLAVOR!

FOR THE MIXTURE :

- 250G | 2 CUPS ALL-PURPOSE FLOUR
- 64G | 3/4 CUP UNSWEETENED COCOA POWDER
- 1 1/4 TSPS BAKING SODA
- 1/2 TSP SALT
- 2 STICKS UNSALTED BUTTER, SOFTENED
- 350G | 1 3/4 CUPS SUGAR
- 2 LARGE EGGS
- 1 TSP PURE VANILLA EXTRACT
- 410ML | 1 1/4 CUPS DRY RED WINE
- POWDERED SUGAR, FOR DUSTING
- WHIPPED CREAM, FOR SERVING

METHOD

STEP 1 PREHEAT THE OVEN TO 175 C / 350 F. GREASE A 12-CUP BUNDT PAN, LIGHTLY FLOUR AND TIP OUT THE EXCESS. WHISK THE FLOUR, COCOA POWDER, BAKING SODA, AND SALT TOGETHER IN A BOWL.

STEP 2 IN A DIFFERENT LARGE BOWL, WHISK TOGETHER THE BUTTER AND SUGAR UNTIL LIGHT AND FLUFFY. GRADUALLY ADD THE EGGS, WHISKING AFTER EACH TIME, UNTIL WELL COMBINED. BEAT IN THE VANILLA FOR TWO MORE MINUTES. BIT BY BIT, FOLD IN THE DRY INGREDIENTS, THEN THE WINE, ALTERNATING UNTIL JUST COMBINED.

STEP 3 SCRAPE THE BATTER INTO THE PAN, BAKE FOR 45 MINS OR UNTIL A STICK COMES OUT CLEAN. ALLOW TO COOL FOR 10 MINS, TURN OUT ONTO A WIRE RACK, THEN ALLOW TO COOL COMPLETELY. SERVE WITH POWDERED SUGAR AND WHIPPED CREAM. ENJOY!

CAKE

NEGRONI COOKIES

PREP TIME: 30 MINS **COOK TIME:** 1 HR 20 MINS **SERVES:** 20

ORANGE NEGRONI COOKIES BEST ENJOYED ALONGSIDE THE CLASSIC COCKTAIL!

FOR THE COOKIE DOUGH:

- 230G | 1 CUP UNSALTED BUTTER, AT ROOM TEMPERATURE
- 1 LARGE EGG
- 1 TSP KOSHER SALT
- 3/4 TSP BAKING SODA
- 250G | 2 CUPS ALL-PURPOSE FLOUR
- 45G | 1/2 CUP UNSWEETENED COCOA

FOR THE ICING:

- 240G | 2 CUPS POWDERED SUGAR
- 4 TO 5 TABLESPOONS CAMPARI, AS NEEDED

ADDITIONAL INGREDIENT:

- WHITE SPARKLING SUGAR (OPTIONAL)

FOR THE SUGAR:

- 400G | 2 CUPS GRANULATED SUGAR
- 2 TSP GRATED ORANGE ZEST (FROM 1 ORANGE)

METHOD ♡

STEP 1 MAKE THE ORANGE SUGAR BY RUBBING THE GRANULATED SUGAR AND ORANGE ZEST WITH YOUR FINGERS UNTIL IT FEELS LIKE WET SAND AND THE COLOR IS EVEN.

STEP 2 PREHEAT THE OVEN TO 175 C / 350 F, WITH A RACK IN BOTH THE UPPER AND LOWER THIRD. PREPARE TWO BAKING TRAYS WITH PARCHMENT PAPER.

STEP 3 IN A LARGE BOWL, BEAT TOGETHER THE BUTTER, EGG, SALT, BAKING SODA AND 300G / 1 1/2 CUPS OF ORANGE SUGAR, UNTIL LIGHT AND FLUFFY. ADD THE FLOUR AND THE COCOA POWDER AND MIX IN UNTIL JUST COMBINED. EVENLY SCOOP THE DOUGH INTO EVEN-SIZED BALLS (AROUND 2 1/2 TBSP). ROLL THE BALLS IN YOUR HANDS.

STEP 4 ROLL THE DOUGH BALLS IN THE ORANGE SUGAR, THEN PUT ON THE BAKING TRAYS AROUND 2 INCHES APART. GENTLY PRESS DOWN WITH YOUR PALM TO FLATTEN TO 3/4 INCH THICKNESS.

STEP 5 BAKE THE COOKIES FOR AROUND 12 MINS, SWAPPING THE TRAYS AROUND FROM TOP TO BOTTOM MIDWAY. LET COOL ON A WIRE RACK.

STEP 6 MAKE THE ICING BY WHISKING THE INGREDIENTS TOGETHER UNTIL SMOOTH. DRIZZLE THE COOKIES WITH THE ICING, THEN GARNISH WITH SPARKLING SUGAR. ALLOW THE ICING TO SOLIDIFY, THEN SERVE AND ENJOY!

STRAWBERRY DAIQUIRI COCKTAIL FANCIES

PREP TIME: 1 HR **COOK TIME:** 30 MINS **SERVES:** 28

TURN YOUR FAVORITE SUMMER COCKTAIL INTO DELICIOUS (AND PINK!) LITTLE FANCIES.

FOR THE CAKES:

- 250G | 8.8 OZ BUTTER, SOFTENED (PLUS EXTRA)
- 4 LARGE EGGS
- 250G | 8.8 OZ GOLDEN CASTER SUGAR
- 250G | 8.8 OZ SELF-RAISING FLOUR
- 1/2 TSP BAKING POWDER
- 1 TSP VANILLA EXTRACT
- 6 TBSP WHITE RUM

FOR THE FILLING:

- 100G | 3.5 OZ BUTTER, SOFTENED
- 100G | 3.5 OZ ICING SUGAR
- 1 TSP MILK
- 6 TSP STRAWBERRY JAM

FOR THE ICING:

- A FEW DROPS PINK FOOD COLORING
- 1KG | 2.2 LB PACK FONDANT ICING SUGAR

TO DECORATE:

- WHITE ICING
- FREEZE-DRIED STRAWBERRIES

METHOD

STEP 1 HEAT THE OVEN TO 180C / 360 F. GREASE AND LINE A 12 X 8-INCH BAKING TIN. ADD ALL OF THE CAKE INGREDIENTS EXCEPT THE WHITE RUM INTO A BOWL AND WHISK UNTIL SMOOTH. POUR THE BATTER INTO THE TIN AND BAKE FOR 30-35 MINS. ALLOW TO COOL COMPLETELY.

STEP 2 WHISK THE FILLING INGREDIENTS (EXCEPT THE JAM) TOGETHER UNTIL SMOOTH, THEN POUR INTO A PIPING BAG.

STEP 3 ONCE THE CAKE HAS COOLED, SLICE OFF THE TOP OF THE CAKE TO FLATTEN IT, THEN DO THE SAME ON THE OTHER SIDE. CUT IN TO 1.5-INCH SQUARES (THERE SHOULD BE 28 IN TOTAL). DIP THEM IN THE RUM THEN PLACE THEM TO SIT WITH SOAKED-SIDE UP. PUT A VERY SMALL DOT OF STRAWBERRY JAM ON THE TOP OF EACH ONE, THEN PIPE A SMALL BALL OF BUTTERCREAM ON TOP (AROUND THE SIZE OF A RASPBERRY).

STEP 4 MIX THE ICING INGREDIENTS WITH SOME WATER - TO MAKE IT A CONDENSED MILK CONSISTENCY. PUT THE SQUARE CAKE ON A WIRE RACK THEN PUT A TRAY UNDERNEATH. ONE BY ONE, PLACE THEM ON A SLOTTED SPOON HELD ABOVE THE ICING BOWL, THEN SPOON OVER THE ICING SUGAR. MOVE OFF THE SPOON USING A KNIFE, THEN LEAVE TO HARDEN ON THE WIRE RACKS. DECORATE WITH THE STRAWBERRIES AND WHITE ICING. ENJOY!

RUM AND ALMOND FRUIT CAKE

PREP TIME: 15 MINS + SOAKING TIME **COOK TIME:** 1 HR 15 MINS **SERVES:** 10

AN EASY FRUITCAKE WITH RUM, IT MAKES A GREAT ADDITION TO CHRISTMAS DINNER.

FOR THE CAKE:

- 100G | 3.5 OZ SULTANAS
- 100G | 3.5 OZ RAISINS
- 50G | 1.7 OZ DARK GLACÉ CHERRIES CHOPPED
- 50G | 1.7 OZ CRYSTALIZED GINGER CHOPPED
- 4 TBSP DARK RUM
- 200G | 7 OZ BUTTER SOFTENED, PLUS MORE FOR THE TIN
- 200G | 7 OZ LIGHT MUSCOVADO SUGAR
- 3 EGGS BEATEN
- 1 TBSP BLACK TREACLE
- 220G | 7.7 OZ SELF-RAISING FLOUR
- 2 TSP MIXED SPICE
- 1 TSP GROUND GINGER
- 1 TSP BAKING POWDER
- 2 SMALL APPLES PEELED AND GRATED

FOR THE ICING:

- 185G | 6.5 OZ SALTED BUTTER AT ROOM TEMPERATURE
- 300G | 10.6 OZ ICING SUGAR
- 1 TSP ALMOND EXTRACT

METHOD

STEP 1 IN A BOWL, ADD THE DRIED FRUITS, GINGER, AND RUM AND ALLOW TO SOAK FOR A FEW HOURS - OR OVERNIGHT. PREHEAT THE OVEN TO 180 C / 360 F. GREASE AN 8-INCH CAKE TIN AND LINE WITH BAKING PAPER. IN A LARGE BOWL COMBINE THE BUTTER, SUGAR, EGGS, TREACLE, SELF-RAISING FLOUR, MIXED SPICE, GROUND GINGER, AND BAKING POWDER UNTIL THICKENED. FOLD IN THE APPLES WITH A LARGE SPOON, AND ADD THE SOAKED FRUIT AND SOAKING LIQUID.

STEP 2 POUR THE BATTER INTO THE TIN, LEVEL AND BAKE FOR 1H 15 MINS, OR UNTIL A STICK COMES OUT CLEAN. ALLOW TO COOL.

STEP 3 BEAT IN THE ICING SUGAR AND ALMOND EXTRACT GRADUALLY TO THE BUTTER UNTIL FLUFFY. SPREAD OVER THE CAKE. SERVE AND ENJOY!

SWEETS

DRUNKEN CHERRY CAKE

PREP TIME: 1 HOUR **COOK TIME:** 1 HOUR **SERVES:** 14

CHOCOLATE CAKE STUFFED WITH DRUNKEN CHERRIES AND CREAM. A TRUE DELIGHT.

FOR THE CAKE:

- 2 X 6 LARGE EGGS
- 2 X 200G | 7 OZ SUGAR
- 2 X 120G | 4.2 OZ ALL-PURPOSE FLOUR
- 2 X 30G | 1.1 OZ COCOA POWDER

FOR THE FRUIT:

- 480ML | 16 OZ VODKA
- 1640G | 58 OZ PITTED CHERRIES IN SYRUP

FOR THE GANACHE:

- 170G | 6 OZ SEMI-SWEET CHOCOLATE CHIPS
- 180ML | 6 OZ WHIPPING CREAM

FOR THE FILLING:

- 720ML | 24 OZ HEAVY WHIPPING CREAM (COLD)
- 200G | 7 OZ SUGAR

METHOD

STEP 1 DRAIN THE JUICE FROM THE CHERRIES AND PLACE INTO A DISH AND COVER IN THE VODKA. COVER WITH PLASTIC WRAP AND ALLOW TO SOAK FOR AT LEAST 8 HOURS, OR OVERNIGHT.

STEP 2 PREHEAT THE OVEN AT 175 F / 350F. TO MAKE THE TWO CAKES, FOLLOW THESE INSTRUCTIONS TWICE. BEAT TOGETHER THE EGGS AND THE SUGAR UNTIL THE BATTER HAS TRIPLED. SIFT IN THE FLOUR AND COCOA POWDER IN TO THE EGG MIX. FOLD IN THE DRY INGREDIENTS WITH A SPATULA, BEING CAREFUL TO MAINTAIN THE FLUFFINESS. POUR INTO A 9-12 INCH ROUND CAKE TIN, GREASED AND LINED. BAKE FOR 30 MINS.

STEP 3 WHEN THE CAKE HAS COOLED, CUT OFF A THIN LAYER FROM EACH SPONGE AND SET ASIDE. CUT A LINE AROUND THE INNER RIM OF THE CAKE AND RIP OUT THE INSIDES TO MAKE A BOWL, SET ASIDE.

STEP 4 IN A MEDIUM BOWL, WHISK THE SUGAR AND WHIPPING CREAM AT A MEDIUM-HIGH SPEED UNTIL THE CREAM FORMS STIFF PEAKS.

STEP 5 DRAIN ALCOHOL FROM THE CHERRIES THEN MIX THE CAKE CRUMBS, CHERRIES AND 80% OF THE CREAM TOGETHER. FILL THE CAKE BOWLS WITH CAKE CREAM, THEN PUT THE SLICED OFF LIDS ON TOP. STACK THE LAYERS TOGETHER WITH SOME CREAM IN BETWEEN, THEN FROST THE OUTSIDE OF THE CAKE. LEAVE IN THE FRIDGE.

STEP 6 PUT THE CHOCOLATE CHIPS IN A BOWL, THEN SIMMER THE CREAM IN A SAUCEPAN - ENSURE IT DOESN'T BOIL. THEN POUR THE CREAM OVER THE CHOCOLATE CHIPS, STIR WELL UNTIL SMOOTH AND MELTED. LET COOL TO ROOM TEMPERATURE. PIPE OR SMOOTH THE GANACHE OVER THE CAKE. DECORATE WITH CHERRIES, PUT IN THE FRIDGE TO SET. SERVE COLD AND ENJOY!

HOLIDAY RUM BALLS

PREP TIME: 35 MINS **COOK TIME:** 5 MINS **SERVES:** 20

TINY BALLS OF RUM AND CHOCOLATE GOODNESS!

FOR THE MIXTURE :

- 230G | 8 OZ STALE CHOCOLATE BROWNIES, CRUMBLED
- 60ML | 1/4 CUP DARK RUM
- 85G | 3 OZ DARK CHOCOLATE, CHOPPED
- 30G | 1 OZ DARK CHOCOLATE, CHOPPED
- 1 TBSP COCOA POWDER, FOR DUSTING

METHOD ♡

STEP 1 SOAK THE CRUMBLED BROWNIES IN RUM FOR 1 MINUTE. MIX UNTIL BECOMES A PASTE-LIKE CONSISTENCY.

STEP 2 USING A 1-INCH SCOOP, SCOOP OUT THE CHOCOLATE-RUM MIX, THEN TRANSFER TO A PLATE LINED WITH PLASTIC WRAP. PLACE THE PLATE IN THE FREEZER FOR 15 - 20 MINS. REMOVE FROM THE FREEZER, ROLL INTO A SMOOTH BALL AND RETURN TO THE FREEZER.

STEP 3 MELT 3 OZ OF CHOCOLATE IN A BOWL OVER SIMMERING WATER, STIRRING FREQUENTLY. ADD THE REMAINING CHOCOLATE, STIRRING UNTIL COMBINED.

STEP 4 REMOVE THE BALLS FROM THE FREEZER, PLACE IN THE MELTED CHOCOLATE AND MOVE AROUND THE COAT COMPLETELY. TRANSFER TO A BAKING MAT, DUST WITH COCOA POWDER AND SERVE. ENJOY!

WHITE CHOCOLATE ROULADE WITH BAILEYS

PREP TIME: 50 MINS **COOK TIME:** 10 MINS **SERVES:** 10

A LUXURIOUS AND SIMPLE ROULADE WHICH IS PERFECT FOR DINNER PARTIES.

FOR THE CAKE:

- 4 EGGS
- 100G | 3.5 OZ GOLDEN CASTER SUGAR PLUS MORE FOR SPRINKLING
- 100G | 3.5 OZ SELF-RAISING FLOUR
- TO DECORATE WHITE PEARLIZED SPRINKLES

FOR THE FILLING:

- 200G | 7 OZ WHITE CHOCOLATE
- 4 TBSP BAILEYS
- 400ML | 14 OZ DOUBLE CREAM

METHOD

STEP 1 PREHEAT THE OVEN TO 200 C / 390 F. LINE A SWISS ROLL TIN WITH BAKING PAPER, ALLOWING AN INCH AT EITHER SIDE.

STEP 2 IN A LARGE BOWL OR STAND MIXER, WHISK TOGETHER THE EGGS AND SUGAR UNTIL PALE AND FLUFFY. SIFT IN THE FLOUR AND GENTLY FOLD, QUICKLY BUT CAREFUL NOT TO REMOVE THE AIR FROM THE MIXTURE. SPOON IT INTO THE TIN AND LEVEL. BAKE FOR 8-10 MINS OR UNTIL FIRM.

STEP 3 ON ANOTHER PIECE OF BAKING PAPER, SPRINKLE WITH CASTER SUGAR, TURN OUT THE SPONGE ON THE SUGAR, THEN ROLL UP IN THE PAPER. ALLOW TO COOL.

STEP 4 IN A BOWL, MELT TOGETHER THE CHOCOLATE AND 2 TBSP OF BAILEYS. ADD 2 TBSP OF CREAM, THEN LEAVE TO SIT FOR A MINUTE, THEN FOLD TOGETHER. IN A DIFFERENT BOWL, WHIP TOGETHER THE REMAINING CREAM INTO STIFF PEAKS, THEN FOLD INTO THE COOLED WHITE CHOCOLATE MIXTURE.

STEP 5 TAKE CARE TO UNROLL THE SPONGE, DO NOT FORCE IT FLAT. BRUSH THE SPONGE WITH BAILEYS, THEN SPREAD SOME OF THE CREAM OVER THE SURFACE, LEAVE HALF AN INCH AT THE EDGES. RE-ROLL THE SPONGE USING THE PAPER. PUT ON A SERVING PLATE SEAM-SIDE DOWN, THEN COVER IN THE REST OF THE CREAM AND SOME SPRINKLES. KEEP CHILLED UNTIL READY TO SERVE. ENJOY!

MARIA'S TIRAMISU CAKE

PREP TIME: 30 MINS **COOK TIME:** 30 MINS **SERVES:** 12

CREAMY, BOOZY AND CHOCOLATEY, YOU HAVE MARIA TO THANK FOR THIS MASTERPIECE!

FOR THE CAKE:

- 300G | 10.5 OZ UNSALTED BUTTER AT ROOM TEMPERATURE
- 270G | 9.5 OZ SELF-RAISING FLOUR
- 1 1/2 TSP BAKING POWDER
- 300G | 10.5 OZ GOLDEN CASTER SUGAR
- 6 EGGS
- 4 TBSP COCOA
- 2 TBSP INSTANT COFFEE DISSOLVED IN 1 TBSP BOILING WATER

FOR THE FILLING:

- 100ML | 3.5 OZ ESPRESSO OR STRONG INSTANT COFFEE COOLED
- 4 TBSP TIA MARIA
- 250ML | 9 OZ TUB MASCARPONE
- 568ML | 20 OZ POT DOUBLE CREAM
- 1 TBSP AMARETTO
- 50G | 1.7 OZ DARK CHOCOLATE

METHOD ♡

STEP 1 PREHEAT THE OVEN TO 180 C / 360 F, GREASE AND LINE TWO 8-INCH CAKE TINS.

STEP 2 IN A FOOD PROCESSOR, BLEND ALL OF THE CAKE INGREDIENTS UNTIL SMOOTH. SPLIT THE MIXTURE BETWEEN THE TWO TINS, THEN COOK FOR 25-30 MINS. ALLOW TO FULLY COOL, THEN CUT EACH IN HALF HORIZONTALLY.

STEP 3 FOR THE FILLING, MIX THE COFFEE AND 2 TBSP OF TIA MARIA, THEN SPRINKLE OVER THE CUT SIDES OF THE CAKES. IN A BOWL, BEAT THE MARSCAPONE SO IT IS SOFTENED, THEN GRADUALLY STIR IN THE CREAM. WHIP IN THE LIQUEURS.

STEP 4 BUILD THE CAKE BY SANDWICHING THE LAYERS TOGETHER USING THE WHIPPED CREAM, RESERVING SOME FOR THE TOP. USE THE LEFT OVER TO TOP WITH A LAYER OF CREAM, AND GRATE OVER DARK CHOCOLATE. CHILL FOR AN HOUR, THEN SERVE. ENJOY!

CAKE

PIMM'S CAKE

PREP TIME: 1 HOUR **COOK TIME:** 30 MINS **SERVES:** 20

TAKE YOUR FAVORITE SUMMER ALCOHOLIC FRUIT CUP AND TURN IT INTO A CAKE!

FOR THE CAKE:

- 1 CUCUMBER
- ZEST AND JUICE OF 1 LEMON
- 300G | 10.5 OZ BUTTER SOFTENED, PLUS EXTRA FOR GREASING
- 300G | 10.5 OZ GOLDEN CASTER SUGAR
- 4 LARGE EGGS
- 1 TSP VANILLA EXTRACT
- 400G | 14 OZ SELF-RAISING FLOUR
- 1 1/2 TSP BAKING POWDER

FOR THE STRAWBERRY BUTTERCREAM:

- 200G | 7 OZ BUTTER SOFTENED
- 500G | 17.6 OZ ICING SUGAR
- 80G | 3 OZ STRAWBERRIES HULLED

FOR THE LEMON BUTTERCREAM:

- 200G | 7 OZ BUTTER SOFTENED
- 400G | 14 OZ POWDERED SUGAR
- JUICE & ZEST 1 LEMON

FOR THE STRAWBERRY FILLING & DECORATION:

- 100G | 3.5 OZ STRAWBERRIES HULLED AND SLICED PLUS 3 STRAWBERRIES, HALVED, (STALKS ON)
- 3 TBSP PIMM'S
- 1/4 CUCUMBER SLICED
- 8 RASPBERRIES

METHOD

STEP 1 IN A BOWL, PUT ALL OF THE STRAWBERRIES FOR DECORATION AND FILLING, AND COVER IN PIMM'S. LEAVE TO SOAK FOR AT LEAST ONE HOUR OR OVERNIGHT FOR A STRONGER FLAVOR.

STEP 2 PREHEAT THE OVEN TO 190C / 375 F, THEN GREASE AND LINE 3 X 8-INCH SANDWICH TINS.

STEP 3 CUT THE CUCUMBER IN HALF LENGTHWAYS, THEN SCRAPE OUT THE SEEDS. CHOP THE CUCUMBER AND ADD TO A BLENDER WITH LEMON JUICE. PUREE.

STEP 4 WHISK THE BUTTER AND SUGAR UNTIL LIGHT AND FLUFFY. ADD ONE EGG AT A TIME, WHISKING IN BETWEEN. ADD THE CUCUMBER PURÉE, LEMON ZEST, AND VANILLA EXTRACT.

STEP 5 ADD THE FLOUR AND BAKING POWDER, FOLDING IN THEN WHISK BRIEFLY SO THERE ARE NO LUMPS. DIVIDE THE MIX BETWEEN THE TINS AND BAKE FOR 30-35 MINS. ALLOW TO COOL IN THE TINS FOR 5 MINS, THEN MOVE TO WIRE RACKS TO COOL FULLY.

STEP 6 IN A BOWL, MASH THE STRAWBERRIES UNTIL MUSHY. IN A LARGER BOWL, WHISK HALF THE POWDERED SUGAR WITH BUTTER UNTIL SMOOTH. THEN WHISK IN THE STRAWBERRIES AND REMAINING POWDERED SUGAR UNTIL SMOOTH. REPEAT WITH THE LEMON BUTTERCREAM AND STORE IN FRIDGE UNTIL NEEDED.

STEP 7 WHEN THE CAKE IS COOL, PUT ONE CAKE ON A STAND AND ADD A THIRD OF THE LEMON BUTTERCREAM, SMOOTH OVER EVENLY, THEN TOP WITH HALF OF THE SOAKED STRAWBERRY SLICES. THEN, SPREAD ONE THIRD OF THE STRAWBERRY BUTTERCREAM OVER ONE OF THE OTHER CAKES, REPEATING THE PROCESS. SANDWICH THE TWO LAYERS TOGETHER, THEN ADD THE FINAL CAKE TO THE TOP.

STEP 8 DECORATE THE REST OF THE CAKE WITH THE REMAINING BUTTERCREAM. PIPE ON THE STRAWBERRY IN RINGS AROUND THE BOTTOM HALF OF THE CAKE, THEN SWITCH TO LEMON HALFWAY UP. SMOOTH OVER WITH A KNIFE TO CREATE A GRADIENT. TOP WITH THE REMAINING SOAKED STRAWBERRIED, RASPBERRIES AND THE CUCUMBER SLICES, THEN SERVE AND ENJOY!

MARGARITA CAKE

PREP TIME: 1 HR 30 MINS **COOK TIME:** 30 MINS **SERVES:** 14

ZESTY AND FRESH, THIS VANILLA CAKE HAS TEQUILA IN TO TAKE IT UP A NOTCH!

FOR THE CAKE

- 390G | 13.8 OZ ALL-PURPOSE FLOUR
- 1/4 TSP BAKING SODA
- 2 3/4 TSP BAKING POWDER
- 1 TSP SALT
- 336G | 11.85 OZ UNSALTED BUTTER, ROOM TEMPERATURE
- 414G | 14.6 OZ SUGAR
- 4 EGG WHITES
- 1 1/2 TSP VANILLA EXTRACT
- 180ML | 6 OZ MILK
- 60ML | 2 OZ LIME JUICE
- 120ML | 4 OZ TEQUILA
- 2 TBSP LIME ZEST

FOR THE DECORATION:

- LIME SLICES
- SUGAR SPRINKLES

FOR THE FROSTING:

- 336G | 11.85 OZ BUTTER
- 336G | 11.85 OZ SHORTENING
- 1380G | 48.7 OZ POWDERED SUGAR
- 1 TBSP FINELY GRATED LIME ZEST
- 6 TBSP FRESH LIME JUICE

METHOD ♡

STEP 1 PREHEAT THE OVEN TO 175 C | 350 F. GREASE THE SIDES OF AND LINE THE BOTTOM OF THREE 8-INCH CAKE PANS.

STEP 2 IN A MEDIUM BOWL, COMBINE THE FLOUR, BAKING SODA, BAKING PWDER AND SALT. IN A LARGE BOWL, WHISK THE BUTTER AND SUGAR TOGETHER UNTIL LIGHT AND FLUFFY.

STEP 3 ADD THE EGG WHITES AND VANILLA TO THE LARGE BOWL AND WHISK IN UNTIL WELL COMBINED, INCLUDING THE SIDES OF THE BOWL. THEN ADD A THIRD OF THE FLOUR MIXTURE, AND WHISK. WHEN COMBINED, ADD THE MILK TO THE BATTER AND WHISK IN, THEN ADD ANOTHER THIRD OF FLOUR AND COMBINE. ADD THE LIME JUICE, TEQUILA AND LIME ZEST, MIX IN, THEN BEAT IN THE REST OF THE DRY INGREDIENTS.

STEP 4 SPLIT THE BATTER BETWEEN THE CAKE PANS AND SMOOTH THE TOPS. BAKE FOR 25-30 MINS, OR UNTIL A STICK COMES OUT CLEAN. ALLOW TO COOK FOR A COUPLE OF MINUTES AND THEN COOL ON A WIRE RACK.

STEP 5 FOR THE FROSTING, BEAT THE BUTTER AND SHORTENING IN A LARGE BOWL UNTIL SMOOTH. GRADUALLY ADD HALF OF THE POWEDERED SUGAR, WHISKING WELL TO COMBINE. ADD THE LIME ZEST AND LIME JUICE, MIX, THEN ADD THE REMAINING POWDERED SUGAR AND COMBINE. IF NEEDED, ADD MORE LIME JUICE TO THIN THE FROSTING.

STEP 6 FOR CONSTRUCTION, CUT OFF THE TOP OF THE CAKES SO THEY ARE FLAT IF NEEDED. PUT ONE CAKE ON A CAKE STAND AND SPREAD WITH AN EVEN LAYER OF ABOUT 1 CUP OF FROSTING. REPEAT WITH THE SECOND LAYER, THEN THE THIRD AND THEN COVER THE CAKE WITH THE FROSTING. DECORATE HOW YOU LIKE WITH LIME SLICES AND SUGAR SPRINKLES. ENJOY!

WHITE RUSSIAN BROWNIE

PREP TIME: 10 MINS **COOK TIME:** 30 MINS **SERVES:** 20

A LUXURIOUS, CREAMY COCKTAIL TURNED INTO LUXURIOUS, CREAMY BROWNIES!

FOR THE BROWNIES:

- 250G | 8 OZ BUTTER
- 350G | 12 OZ DARK CHOCOLATE CHIPS
- 325G | 11.5 OZ SELF-RAISING FLOUR
- 1/2 TSP BAKING POWDER
- 100G | 3.5 OZ TOASTED HAZELNUTS
- 325G | 11 OZ LIGHT MUSCOVADO SUGAR
- 2 LARGE EGGS
- 60ML | 2 OZ KAHLÚA OR COFFEE-FLAVORED LIQUEUR
- 60ML | 2 OZ VODKA

FOR THE SYRUP:

- 3 TBSP KAHLÚA
- 3 TBSP VODKA
- COCOA POWDER, TO DUST
- WHIPPED CREAM

METHOD

STEP 1 PREHEAT THE OVEN TO 180 C / 355 F, THEN GREASE AND LINE A 9-INCH PAN.

STEP 2 OVER A PAN OF SIMMERING WATER, PLACE A HEAT-SAFE BOWL THEN ADD THE BUTTER AND CHOCOLATE AND STIR UNTIL MELTED. REMOVE FROM THE HEAT TO COOL. IN A LARGE BOWL, SIFT IN THE FLOUR, BAKING POWDER AND SALT, THEN ADD THE HAZELNUTS.

STEP 3 IN A NEW BOWL, WHISK THE EGGS AND MUSCOVADO SUGAR UNTIL CREAMY. THEN ADD IN THE KAHLÚA, VODKA AND CHOCOLATE MIXTURE, THEN MIX IN WELL. ADD THE DRY INGREDIENTS AND FOLD UNTIL JUST INCORPORATED. TRANSFER THE MIXTURE TO THE BAKING PAN, THEN BAKE FOR 30 MINS. A STICK MAY NOT COME OUT FULLY CLEAN, BUT THE BROWNIES WILL FIRM AS THEY COOL.

STEP 4 TO SERVE, BRUSH OVER THE EXTRA KAHLÚA WHILST STILL WARM. THEN SERVE AS SQUARES WITH WHIPPED CREAM AND COCOA POWDER. ENJOY!

PIÑA COLADA KEY LIME PIE

PREP TIME: 20 MINS **COOK TIME:** 30 MINS **SERVES:** 8

BOOZY, COCONUTTY AND ZESTY, THIS PIE IS A REAL TREAT.

FOR THE PIE:

- 350G | 12.3 OZ COCONUT BISCUITS
- 150G | 5.3 OZ BUTTER, MELTED
- 3 EGG YOLKS
- 5 TBSP COCONUT RUM
- 400G | 14 OZ TIN CONDENSED MILK
- 4 LIMES, ZESTED AND JUICED
- 300ML | 10.1 OZ DOUBLE CREAM
- 2 TBSP ICING SUGAR

TO FINISH:

- TOASTED COCONUT SHREDS

METHOD

STEP 1 PREHEAT THE OVEN TO 160 C / 320 F. IN A FOOD PROCESSOR, CRUMBLE IN THE BISCUITS AND BLITZ TO CRUMBS. TRANSFER TO A BOWL, THEN MIX WITH MELTED BUTTER. IN AN 8-INCH LOOSE-BOTTOMED SPONGE TIN, PRESS THE BISCUIT MIXTURE INTO THE BASE AND SIDES. BAKE FOR 10 MINS, THEN ALLOW TO COOL.

STEP 2 IN A BOWL, WHISK TOGETHER THE EGG YOLKS AND 3 TBSP OF RUM UNTIL PALE. ADD THE CONDENSED MILK, THEN WHISK FOR 4 MORE MINUTES. ADD THE LIME ZEST AND JUICE, THEN WHISK FOR A COUPLE OF MINUTES UNTIL THICKENED.

STEP 3 POUR THE MIXTURE ON TOP OF THE BISCUIT, THEN BAKE FOR 20 MINS. ALLOW TO COOL THEN PUT IN THE FRIDGE FOR 2-3 HOURS, UNTIL COMPLETELY CHILLED.

STEP 4 FOR THE TOPPING, WHISK THE CREAM, ICING SUGAR AND 2 TBSP OF RUM IN A BOWL. WHEN SOFTLY WHIPPED, PILE ON TOP OF THE PIE AND SCATTER OVER COCONUT SHREDS.

WHISKEY CARAMEL AND BANANA SELF-SAUCING PUDDING

PREP TIME: 15 MINS **COOK TIME:** 40 MINS **SERVES:** 8

WARMING, SPIKED WITH WHISKEY AND SUPER SAUCY, THIS MAKES A DELICIOUS AUTUMN TREAT.

FOR THE PUDDINGS:

- 175G | 6.2 OZ PLAIN FLOUR
- 100G | 3.5 OZ GOLDEN CASTER SUGAR
- 1 TBSP BAKING POWDER
- 2 VERY RIPE BANANAS, MASHED, PLUS 1 WHOLE BANANA, SLICED
- 300ML | 10.1 OZ WHOLE MILK
- 85G | 3 OZ UNSALTED BUTTER, MELTED, PLUS EXTRA FOR THE BAKING DISH
- 1 EGG, BEATEN
- 1 TSP VANILLA EXTRACT OR PASTE

FOR THE SAUCE:

- 150G | 5.3 OZ SOFT DARK BROWN SUGAR
- 4 TBSP GOLDEN SYRUP
- 2 TBSP WHISKEY

TO SERVE:

- ICE CREAM OR CUSTARD

METHOD

STEP 1 PREHEAT THE OVEN TO 180 C / 355 F. IN A LARGE BOWL, MIX TOGETHER THE FLOUR, SUGAR, BAKING POWDER, AND A PINCH OF SALT.

STEP 2 IN A DIFFERENT BOWL OR JUG, WHISK TOGETHER THE REST OF THE PUDDING INGREDIENTS TOGETHER UNTIL WELL COMBINED. THEN GRADUALLY POUR IN THE LIQUID MIXTURE TO THE FLOUR MIX, WHISKING AS YOU GO. GREASE A 3-INCH DEEP, 10-INCH WIDE PAN, THEN POUR IN THE BATTER.

STEP 3 IN A SMALL PAN, HEAT THE SUGAR, GOLDEN SYRUP, AND 8.8OZ OF JUST-BOILED WATER, UNTIL SMOOTH. SIMMER, THEN REMOVE FROM THE HEAT AND ADD THE WHISKEY.

STEP 4 POUR THE SAUCE OVER THE PUDDING, DECORATE WITH SLICED BANANAS, THEN BAKE FOR 40-45 MINS. SERVE HOT WITH YOUR CHOICE OF ICE CREAM OR CUSTARD. ENJOY!

GIN AND TONIC CAKE

PREP TIME: 30 MINS **COOK TIME:** 1 HOUR **SERVES:** 8

FRESH AND CITRUSSY, THIS IS THE PERFECT CAKE FOR G&T LOVERS!

FOR THE CAKE:

- 200G | 7 OZ UNSALTED BUTTER, PLUS EXTRA FOR GREASING
- 200G | 7 OZ GOLDEN CASTER SUGAR
- 4 LARGE EGGS
- 175G | 6.2 OZ PLAIN FLOUR
- 75G | 2.6 OZ FULL-FAT LEMON YOGURT
- 100G | 3.5 OZ SELF-RAISING FLOUR
- 3 TBSP GIN
- 3 LEMONS, ZESTED (JUICE USED IN SYRUP)

FOR THE SYRUP:

- 5 LEMONS, JUICED, PLUS 2 SMALL LEMONS, SLICED (DISCARD END SLICES)
- 125G | 4.4 OZ GOLDEN CASTER SUGAR
- 12 JUNIPER BERRIES
- 6 TBSP TONIC WATER
- 2 TBSP GIN

METHOD

STEP 1 PREHEAT THE OVEN TO 160 C / 320 F. GREASE AND LINE A 9X5-INCH TIN. IN A LARGE BOWL, WHISK TOGETHER THE BUTTER, SUGAR, AND A PINCH OF SALT UNTIL LIGHT AND FLUFFY. ADD THE EGGS ONE BY ONE, WHISKING WELL INBETWEEN. FOR THE LAST TWO EGGS, ADD A TBSP OF PLAIN FLOUR. ADD THE LEMON YOGHURT, BEAT WELL, THEN FOLD IN THE FLOUR WITH A LARGE METAL SPOON. ADD THE GIN AND LEMON ZEST AND FOLD IN. TRANSFER TO THE CAKE TIN AND BAKE FOR 1 HOUR, UNTIL RISEN AND GOLDEN.

STEP 2 IN A WIDE PAN, ADD THE JUICE FROM THE 8 LEMONS, SUGAR, JUNIPER BERRIES AND TONIC WATER, THEN HEAT GENTLY UNTIL THE SUGAR DISSOLVES. ADD THE LEMON SLICE FOR 3 MINUTES, THEN REMOVE FROM THE HEAT, ADD THE GIN AND STIR.

STEP 3 ALLOW THE CAKE TO COOL FOR 10 MINS, THEN TURN IT OUT ONTO A PLATE. POKE SOME HOLES IN THE BASE USING A SKEWER OR FORK, THEN SPOON HALF OF THE SYRUP OVER THE BASE TO SOAK IN.

STEP 4 TURN THE CAKE THE RIGHT WAY UP, THEN SPOON OVER THE REST OF THE SYRUP AND DECORATE WITH THE LEMON SLICES. LET IT SOAK IN BEFORE ADDING MORE. SERVE AND ENJOY!

MIMOSA CUPCAKES

PREP TIME: 30 MINS **COOK TIME:** 21 MINS **SERVES:** 15

WITH THE TASTE OF BRUNCH, MAKE THESE FOR YOUR AFTERNOON TEA INSTEAD!

FOR THE CUPCAKES:

- 207G | 7.3 OZ CAKE FLOUR, SPOONED & LEVELED
- 1/2 TSP BAKING POWDER
- 1/4 TSP BAKING SODA
- 1/4 TSP SALT
- 113G | 4 OZ UNSALTED BUTTER, SOFTENED TO ROOM TEMPERATURE
- 200G | 7 OZ GRANULATED SUGAR
- 3 LARGE EGG WHITES
- 1 TSP PURE VANILLA EXTRACT
- 1 1/2 TBSP ORANGE ZEST
- 80G | 2.8 OZ FULL-FAT SOUR CREAM
- 30ML | 1 OZ JUICE FROM AN ORANGE
- 120ML | 4 OZ CHAMPAGNE

FOR THE FROSTING:

- 180ML | 6 OZ CHAMPAGNE
- 226G | 8 OZ UNSALTED BUTTER, SOFTENED TO ROOM TEMPERATURE
- 480G | 17 OZ POWDERED SUGAR
- 1 TSP PURE VANILLA EXTRACT

TO GARNISH:

- ORANGE SLICES
- GOLD SPRINKLES

METHOD

STEP 1 PREHEAT THE OVEN TO 175 C / 350 F. LINE A CUPCAKE TRAY WITH 15 CASES - OR USE TWO 12-CUP PANS.

STEP 2 IN A LARGE BOWL ADD THE FLOUR, BAKING POWDER, BAKING SODA, AND SALT. THEN IN A DIFFERENT BOWL BEAT TOGETHER THE BUTTER AND SUGAR UNTIL CREAMY. ADD THE EGG WHITES AND VANILLA, BEAT TOGETHER AGAIN, THEN BEAT IN THE ORANGE ZEST AND SOUR CREAM. THEN GRADUALLY ADD THE FLOUR MIX, MIXING AT A LOW SPEED UNTIL JUST COMBINED. AT A LOW SPEED AGAIN, SLOWLY MIX IN THE ORANGE JUICE AND CHAMPAGNE, TAKING CARE TO NOT OVERMIX.

STEP 3 POUR THE MIX INTO THE LINERS, FILLING UP TO 2/3 FULL. BAKE FOR 18-21 MINS, THEN ALLOW TO COOL FULLY.

STEP 4 FOR THE FROSTING, ADD THE CHAMPAGNE TO A SMALL SAUCEPAN AND THEN BRING TO THE BOIL. REDUCE THE HEAT AND SIMMER UNTIL REDUCE 1/4 CUP, OR FOR ABOUT 7-10 MINS. ALLOW TO COOL TO ROOM TEMPERATURE OR COLD.

STEP 5 IN A LARGE BOWL, WHISK THE BUTTER UNTIL CREAMY, THEN ADD THE POWDERED SUGAR GRADUALLY, INCORPORATING WELL EACH TIME BEFORE ADDING MORE. WHEN WELL COMBINED, WHISK IN 3 TBSP OF THE CHAMPAGNE SYRUP, AND ADD VANILLA EXTRACT. ADD MORE OF THE REDUCED CHAMPAGNE IF DESIRED. FROST THE CUPCAKES, GARNISH AND SERVE. ENJOY!

FROZEN MAI TAI CAKE

PREP TIME: 15 MINS **COOK TIME:** FREEZE OVERNIGHT **SERVES:** 10

A FROZEN DELIGHT, YOU'LL WANT TO EAT THIS ON THE BEACH!

FOR THE BASE:

- 180G | 1 1/2 CUPS VANILLA WAFER COOKIES, CRUSHED (ABOUT 40 COOKIES)
- 6 TBSP BUTTER, MELTED

FOR THE FILLING:

- 2 PINTS MANGO SORBET, SOFTENED
- 227G | 2 CANS (8 OZ EACH) EACH CRUSHED PINEAPPLE, UNDRAINED
- 5 TBSP GOLD RUM
- 2 TBSP LIME JUICE
- 2 TBSP MARASCHINO CHERRY JUICE

OPTIONAL GARNISH:

- THINLY SLICED LIMES
- MARASCHINO CHERRIES

METHOD

STEP 1 GREASE A 9-INCH SPRINGFORM PAN. IN A BOWL, MIX THE COOKIE CRUMBS AND BUTTER TOGETHER, THEN PRESS INTO THE BOTTOM OF THE PAN.

STEP 2 BLEND TOGETHER THE SORBET, PINEAPPLE, RUM, AND LIME JUICE IN A FOOD PROCESSOR. SET ASIDE 1/3 INTO A SMALL BOWL, THEN ADD THE MARASCHINO CHERRY JUICE AND STIR.

STEP 3 POUR THE MANGO MIXTURE INTO A PAN, THEN ADD THE CHERRY MIX. SWIRL THE FILLINGS TOGETHER WITH A KNIFE. FREEZE OVERNIGHT.

STEP 4 15 MINUTES BEFORE SERVING, REMOVE THE CAKE FROM THE FREEZER. TOP WITH LIME AND MARASCHINO CHERRIES, THEN SERVE AND ENJOY!

SWEETS

JÄGERMEISTER AND HONEY BUNDT CAKE

PREP TIME: 20 MINS **COOK TIME:** 40 MINS **SERVES:** 12

SWEET LIKE HONEY, THIS IS A GREAT BOOZY BUNDT CAKE FOR CHRISTMAS!

FOR THE CAKE:

- 280G | 9.9 OZ ALL-PURPOSE FLOUR
- 2 TSP BAKING SODA
- 2 TSP GROUND GINGER
- 2 TSP GROUND CINNAMON
- 1/2 TSP GROUND CLOVES
- 1/2 TSP SALT
- 226G | 8 OZ UNSALTED BUTTER (2 STICKS)
- 200G | 7 OZ PACKED LIGHT BROWN SUGAR
- 2 LARGE EGGS
- 340G | 12 OZ HONEY
- 120ML | 4 OZ JÄGERMEISTER
- 180ML | 6 OZ HOT WATER

FOR THE GLAZE:

- 80ML | 2.7 OZ JÄGERMEISTER
- 57G | 2 OZ UNSALTED BUTTER (1/2 STICK)
- POWDERED SUGAR FOR DUSTING

METHOD

STEP 1 PREHEAT THE OVEN TO 175 F / 350 C, THEN GREASE THE BUNDT PAN. IN A BOWL, COMBINE THE FLOUR, BAKING SODA, GINGER, CINNAMON, CLOVES, AND SALT.

STEP 2 IN A DIFFERENT LARGE BOWL, BEAT TOGETHER THE BROWN SUGAR AND BUTTER. THEN ADD THE EGGS ONE AT A TIME, MIXING WELL AFTER EACH, THEN MIX IN THE HONEY AND JÄGER. ADD THE FLOUR MIXTURE AND FOLD IN, THEN MIX IN THE HOT WATER WELL. POUR THE BATTER INTO THE BUNDT PAN.

STEP 3 BAKE IN THE OVEN FOR 40-45 MINS, THEN ALLOW TO COOL FOR 15 MINS.

STEP 4 WHILST THE CAKE IS COOKING, MAKE THE GLAZE BY MELTING THE BUTTER IN A SAUCEPAN, THEN REMOVE FROM THE HEAT AND MIX IN THE JÄGER. BRUSH THE SAUCE ON THE BOTTOM OF THE CAKE AND ALLOW TO SOAK IN FOR 5 MINUTES.

STEP 5 FLIP THE CAKE ON A SERVING PLATE, COVER IN THE REST OF THE GLAZE AND LET COOL. DUST WITH POWDERED SUGAR, AND SERVE. ENJOY!

RUM BANANA BREAD

PREP TIME: 20 MINS **COOK TIME:** 1 HR 15 MINS **SERVES:** 10

A CARIBBEAN TWIST ON THE CLASSIC BANANA BREAD, THIS WILL BECOME YOUR GO-TO!

FOR THE FILLING:

- 3 LARGE OVERRIPE BANANAS, MASHED
- 120G | 4.2 OZ BROWN SUGAR, PACKED
- 115G | 4 OZ UNSALTED BUTTER PLUS EXTRA FOR GREASING
- 45ML | 1.5 OZ DARK RUM OR SPICED RUM
- 2 LARGE EGGS, ROOM TEMPERATURE
- 60ML | 2 OZ VEGETABLE OIL
- 60ML | 2 OZ SOUR CREAM, ROOM TEMPERATURE
- 60ML | 2 OZ BUTTERMILK, ROOM TEMPERATURE
- 1 TSP VANILLA EXTRACT
- 240G | 8.5 OZ FLOUR, SPOONED AND LEVELED
- 135G | 4.8 OZ GRANULATED SUGAR
- 1 TSP BAKING SODA
- 1/2 TSP GROUND NUTMEG
- 1/2 TSP SALT
- 1/4 TSP CINNAMON
- 1/4 TSP CARDAMOM

FOR THE GLAZE:

- 120G | 4.2 OZ POWDERED SUGAR
- 15-30ML | 0.5-1 OZ RUM
- 30G | 1 OZ UNSALTED BUTTER, MELTED

METHOD

STEP 1 PREHEAT THE OVEN TO 175 F / 350 F. PUT THE OVEN RACK TO THE LOWER THIRD POSITION.

STEP 2 GREASE AN 8.5 X 4.5-INCH LOAF PAN, THEN LIGHTLY FLOUR AND DISTRIBUTE EVENLY. TAP TO REMOVE EXCESS.

STEP 3 IN A PAN, MIX THE MASHED BANANAS, BUTTER, BROWN SUGAR, AND RUM. WHISK WHILST COOKING OVER A MEDIUM HEAT TO MELT THE BUTTER. WHEN IT BEGINS TO SIMMER, TURN THE HEAT DOWN THEN SIMMER FOR 3-5 MINS, MIXING OCCASIONALLY. REMOVE FROM THE HEAT AND ALLOW TO COOL FOR 10 MINS.

STEP 4 COMBINE THE EGGS, OIL, SOUR CREAM, BUTTERMILK, AND VANILLA EXTRACT IN A LARGE BOWL, THEN ADD THE BANANA MIX AND WHISK TOGETHER. IN A DIFFERENT BOWL, MIX TOGETHER THE FLOUR, SUGAR, BAKING SODA, SALT, NUTMEG, CINNAMON, AND CARDAMOM. FOLD TOGETHER THE DRY AND WET INGREDIENTS, TAKING CARE TO NOT OVERMIX.

STEP 5 POUR THE BATTER INTO THE PAN, THEN BAKE FOR 60-65 MINS. IN A BOWL, WHISK THE POWDERED SUGAR, RUM AND BUTTER TOGETHER. ADD MORE OR LESS RUM AND SUGAR TO YOUR TASTE AND DESIRED CONSISTENCY. WHEN THE BREAD HAS COOLED, COVER IN THE FROSTING. SERVE AND ENJOY!

AMARETTI & SULTANA CHEESECAKE

PREP TIME: 20 MINS COOK TIME: 35 MINS SERVES: 10

A CREAMY ALMOND DELIGHT, THE AMARETTO PERFECTLY COMPLEMENTS THIS CHEESECAKE!

FOR THE MIXTURE :

- 100G | 3.5 OZ SULTANAS
- 3 TBSP AMARETTO PLUS EXTRA TO SERVE, OPTIONAL
- 50G | 1.8 OZ BUTTER PLUS EXTRA FOR GREASING
- 6 DIGESTIVE BISCUITS, CRUSHED TO CRUMBS
- 8 AMARETTI BISCUITS, CRUSHED TO CRUMBS
- 600G | 21.2 OZ FULL-FAT CREAM CHEESE (2 X 300G PACKS)
- 3 EGGS
- 170G | 6 OZ SOURED CREAM (1 POT)
- 3 TBSP SELF-RAISING FLOUR
- 1 TSP VANILLA EXTRACT
- 175G | 6.2 OZ GOLDEN CASTER SUGAR
- ICING SUGAR, TO SERVE
- ROUGHLY BROKEN AMARETTI BISCUITS, TO SERVE

METHOD

STEP 1 IN A BOWL, COVER THE SULTANAS WITH THE AMARETTO AND LEAVE TO SOAK FOR AN HOUR. PREHEAT THE OVEN TO 180 C / 355 F, AND GREASE A 9-INCH ROUND CAKE TIN. IN A SAUCEPAN, GENTLY MELT THE BUTTER THEN STIR IN THE BISCUIT CRUMBS. COAT IN THE BUTTER, THEN POUR INTO THE TIN AND PRESS DOWN TO PACK IN. BAKE FOR 5 MINS THEN ALLOW TO COOL.

STEP 2 IN A LARGE BOWL, BEAT THE CHEESE, EGGS, SOURED CREAM, FLOUR, VANILLA, AND CASTER SUGAR UNTIL SMOOTH. STIR IN THE SOAKED SULTANAS AND ANY REMAINING AMARETTO, THEN COVER THE BASE. SMOOTH.

STEP 3 BAKE FOR 30 MINS THEN ALLOW TO COOL IN THE TIN. SERVE CHILLED, CAREFULLY TURN OUT THE CAKE AND TOP WITH ICING AND BROKEN AMARETTI BUSCUITS. ENJOY!

CLASSIC SHERRY TRIFLE

PREP TIME: 45 MINS COOK TIME: 15 MINS SERVES: 10

A CHRISTMAS STAPLE FOR MANY, THIS IS YOUR CLASSIC FESTIVE TRIFLE.

FOR THE MIXTURE :

- 750G | 26.5 OZ FROZEN SUMMER FRUITS
- 250G | 8.8 OZ CASTER SUGAR
- 9 SHEETS LEAF GELATINE
- 75G | 2.6 OZ CUSTARD POWDER
- 1.2 LITRES | 40.6 OZ MILK
- 1 1/2 - 2 MADEIRA CAKES
- 4 TBSP SHERRY OR CASSIS
- 300-450ML | 10.1-15.2 OZ DOUBLE CREAM
- 1 TSP VANILLA EXTRACT
- 2 TBSP ICING SUGAR
- 2 CRUSHED AMARETTI BISCUITS, TO SERVE

METHOD ♡

STEP 1 IN A SAUCEPAN, ADD THE FROZEN FRUIT, 200G / 7 OZ OF CASTER SUGAR AND A LITER / 34 OZ OF WATER. BRING TO A SIMMER, THEN SIMMER FOR 2 MINS. REMOVE 6 TBSP OF THE FRUIT, AND 150ML / 5 OZ OF THE JUICE, THEN ALLOW TO SIMMER FOR A FURTHER 5 MINS.

STEP 2 IN A DIFFERENT BOWL, SOAK THE LEAF GELATINE IN COLD WATER. IN THE PAN, BLITZ OR MASH THE FRUIT, THEN STRAIN THROUGH A SIEVE INTO A LARGE BOWL. PUSH THE PULP THROUGH THE SIEVE SO ONLY THE SKINS AND SEEDS REMAIN.

STEP 3 REMOVE THE GELATINE FROM THE WATER AND SQUEEZE OUT ANY EXCESS. ADD THE GELATINE TO THE FRUIT JUICE BOWL, AND STIR UNTIL DISSOLVED. COOL THE MIXTURE, THEN CHILL IN THE FRIDGE UNTIL ALMOST SET.

STEP 4 MAKE THE CUSTARD AS PER THE INSTRUCTIONS USING THE CUSTARD POWDER, MILK, AND CASTER SUGAR. THE CUSTARD WILL BE VERY THICK. COVER WITH BAKING POWDER AND ALLOW TO SLIGHTLY COOL.

STEP 5 IN A TRIFLE BOWL, PILE IN THE MADEIRA CAKES, SPOON OVER THE REST OF THE JUICE AND BERRIES, AND ADD THE SHERRY. POUR IN THE CUSTARD ON TOP, PUSHING IT AGAINST THE SIDES TO SEAL IN THE CAKE. ALLOW TO COOL AND SET WITH A SKIN. ONCE COLD, SPOON THE JELLY OVER, THEN CHILL UNTIL READY TO COMPLETE.

STEP 6 WHIP THE DOUBLE CREAM, VANILLA EXTRACT, AND ICING SUGAR TOGETHER UNTIL JUST HOLDING SHAPE, THEN SPOON AROUND THE BOWL ON TOP OF THE JELLY. SCATTER WITH THE SERVING BISCUITS, CHILL THEN SERVE WHEN READY. ENJOY!

MINT BAILEYS BARS

PREP TIME: 25 MINS **COOK TIME:** 45 MINS **SERVES:** 64

LITTLE MINTY BOOZY BROWNIES THAT WILL LEAVE YOU WANTING MORE!

FOR THE MIXTURE:

- 170G | 6 OZ BUTTER, CUBED
- 170G | 6 OZ DARK CHOCOLATE CHIPS
- 150G | 5.3 OZ SUGAR
- 2 LARGE EGGS PLUS 1 LARGE EGG YOLK, ROOM TEMPERATURE
- 1 TSP VANILLA EXTRACT
- 120G | 4.2 OZ ALL-PURPOSE FLOUR
- 40G | 1.4 OZ DARK BAKING COCOA
- 1/2 TSP SALT
- 1 CUP ANDES CREME DE MENTHE BAKING CHIPS

FOR THE TOPPING:

- 225G | 8 OZ CREAM CHEESE, SOFTENED
- 100G | 3.5 OZ SUGAR
- 60ML | 2 OZ IRISH CREAM LIQUEUR, SUCH AS BAILEYS
- 1 LARGE EGG PLUS 1 LARGE EGG WHITE, ROOM TEMPERATURE

METHOD

STEP 1 PREHEAT THE OVEN TO 175 C / 350 F, GREASE AND LINE AN 8-INCH SQUARE PAN, LETTING ENDS EXTEND UP THE SIDES. MELT THE BUTTER AND CHOCOLATE IN A HEAT-PROOF BOWL IN EITHER MICROWAVE OR OVER A DOUBLE BROILER.

STEP 2 STIR WELL. ADD THE SUGAR AND WHISK. ALLOW TO COOL SLIGHTLY THEN WHISK IN THE EGGS AND EXTRA YOLK ONE BY ONE. ADD THE VANILLA AND MIX UNTIL BLENDED. FOLD IN THE FLOUR, BAKING COCOA, SALT, THEN THE ANDES CHIPS. POUR INTO PAN.

STEP 3 IN A LARGE BOWL BEAT TOGETHER THE CREAM CHEESE AND SUGAR UNTIL SMOOTH, THEN MIX IN THE LIQUEUR.

STEP 4 ADD THE EGG AND EGG WHITE, WHISKING SLOWLY UNTIL COMBINED. POUR THE TOPPING OVER THE BROWNIE MIX.

STEP 5 BAKE FOR 45 MINS, THEN COOL FOR AN HOUR ON A WIRE RACK. LEAVE IN THE FRIDGE FOR AT LEAST 3 HOURS.

STEP 6 REMOVE THE BROWNIES BY USING THE EXCESS PAPER, CUT INTO SQUARES, SERVE AND ENJOY!

LEMON VODKA DRIZZLE CAKE

PREP TIME: 15 MINS **COOK TIME:** 40 MINS **SERVES:** 10

A VODKA SPIKED TWIST ON THE CLASSIC DRIZZLE OR POUND CAKE, THIS IS PERFECT FOR RAINY AFTERNOONS!

FOR THE MIXTURE :

- 170G | 6 OZ BUTTER
- 170G | 6 OZ GOLDEN CASTER SUGAR (PLUS 30G | 1 OZ FOR DRIZZLE)
- 3 EGGS
- 170G | 6 OZ SELF-RAISING FLOUR, SIFTED
- 1 TSP BAKING POWDER
- ZEST AND JUICE OF 1 LARGE LEMON
- 20ML | 0.7 OZ VODKA (A SPLASH OR TWO)

METHOD

STEP 1 PREHEAT THE OVEN TO 170 C / 340 F. BEAT TOGETHER THE SUGAR AND BUTTER IN A BOWL UNTIL CREAMY. ADD THE EGGS ONE AT A TIME, ADDING A SPOONFUL OF FLOUR AND BEATING WELL AFTER EACH. FOLD THROUGH THE REST OF THE FLOUR.

STEP 2 MIX IN THE LEMON ZEST AND 2 TBSP OF LEMON JUICE, THEN POUR THE MIXTURE INTO A LINED AND GREASED LOAF TIN. BAKE FOR 40 MINS, THEN CHECK WITH A STICK TO SEE IF COMES OUT CLEAN. IF IT DOESN'T, COOK FOR 5 MINS, CHECK, THEN CONTINUE UNTIL READY. DO NOT OPEN THE OVEN BEFORE 40 MINS OR YOUR CAKE MAY COLLAPSE.

STEP 3 MEANWHILE, HEAT THE REST OF THE LEMON JUICE, SUGAR, AND VODKA TOGETHER UNTIL THE SUGAR IS DISSOLVED AND IT IS SYRUPY. POUR OVER THE HOT CAKE, AND LEAVE TO COOL BEFORE REMOVING FROM THE TIN. SERVE AND ENJOY!

FIREBALL PUMPKIN PIE

PREP TIME: 25 MINS **COOK TIME:** 50 MINS **SERVES:** 8

A SPICY AND FIERY PUMPKIN PIE THAT PUTS ALL OTHERS TO SHAME!

FOR THE MIXTURE :

- DOUGH FOR SINGLE-CRUST PIE
- 2 LARGE EGGS
- 425G | 15 OZ CANNED PUMPKIN
- 240ML | 8 OZ HALF-AND-HALF CREAM
- 150G | 5.3 OZ SUGAR
- 55G | 1.9 OZ PACKED BROWN SUGAR
- 3 TBSP FIREBALL CINNAMON WHISKEY
- 1/2 TSP PUMPKIN PIE SPICE
- 1/4 TSP SALT

METHOD

STEP 1 PREHEAT THE OVEN TO 220 C / 425 F. LIGHTLY FLOUR A SURFACE AND THEN ROLL THE DOUGH INTO A 1/8 -INCH CIRCLE. PUT IN 9-INCH PIE DISH. TRIM THE CRUST SO ONLY 1/2 INCH HANGS OVER. FLUTE THE EDGE.

STEP 2 IN A LARGE BOWL, MIX TOGETHER THE EGGS, PUMPKIN, CREAM, SUGARS, WHISKEY, PUMPKIN PIE SPICE, AND SALT UNTIL SMOOTH. FILL THE CRUST WITH THE FILLING.

STEP 3 BAKE IN THE OVEN FOR 15 MINS, THEN REDUCE THE HEAT TO 175 C / 350 F. BAKE FOR A FURTHER 45 MINS, UNTIL THE CRUST IS GOLDEN BROWN.

STEP 4 COVER THE EDGES WITH FOIL IF NEEDED TO STOP BROWNING.

STEP 5 REMOVE FROM OVEN AND COOL ON A WIRE RACK FOR 1 HR, THEN CHILL IN THE FRIDGE OVERNIGHT OR UNTIL SET. SERVE AND ENJOY!

LIMONCELLO TIRAMISU

PREP TIME: 15 MINS **COOK TIME:** 15 MINS **SERVES:** 16

A FAR-CRY FROM THE TRADITIONAL TIRAMISU, THIS BOOZY CITRUSSY VERSION IS EVEN BETTER!

FOR THE MIXTURE:

- 100G | 3.5 OZ SUGAR
- 60ML | 2 OZ WATER
- 2 TBSP LIMONCELLO

FOR THE CURD:

- 300G | 10.5 OZ SUGAR
- 45G | 1.6 OZ CORNSTARCH
- 360ML | 12.2 OZ COLD WATER
- 3 LARGE EGG YOLKS, LIGHTLY BEATEN
- 3 TBSP BUTTER, CUBED
- 120ML | 4 OZ LEMON JUICE
- 2 TSP GRATED LEMON ZEST

FOR ASSEMBLY:

- 3 PACKAGES (85G EACH) LADYFINGERS, SPLIT
- 4 MACAROON COOKIES, CRUMBLED
- CANDIED LEMON PEEL, OPTIONAL

METHOD

STEP 1 BOIL TOGETHER THE SUGAR AND WATER IN A SMALL SAUCEPAN. STIR UNTIL THE SUGAR IS DISSOLVED. REMOVE FROM THE HEAT THEN STIR IN THE LIMONCELLO. REMOVE FROM HEAT.

STEP 2 TO MAKE THE LEMON CURD, IN A DIFFERENT SAUCEPAN, COMBINE THE SUGAR AND THE CORNSTARCH. ADD WATER AND STIR UNTIL SMOOTH. BOIL AND STIR FOR ABOUT 1 MIN UNTIL THICK. REMOVE FROM HEAT.

STEP 3 STIR SOME OF THE HOT MIXTURE INTO THE EGG YOLKS, THEN MOVE ALL INTO THE PAN AGAIN, CONTINUALLY STIRRING. BRING THE MIXTURE TO A GENTLE BOIL AND CONTINUE TO STIR FOR 2 MORE MINUTES. REMOVE FROM THE HEAT, ADD THE BUTTER AND STIR. STIR IN THE LEMON JUICE AND ZEST, THEN SET ASIDE ALLOW TO COOL TO ROOM TEMP.

STEP 4 BEAT THE CREAM UNTIL IT THICKENS IN A LARGE BOWL, THEN ADD THE SUGAR AND CONTINUE TO BEAT UNTIL FORMS STIFF PEAKS. FOLD IN THE MARSCAPONE AND WHIPPED CREAM INTO THE COOLED LEMON CURD MIXTURE.

STEP 5 IN A 9-INCH SPRINGFORM PAN, ARRANGE A THIRD OF THE LADYFINGERS. COVER WITH A THIRD OF THE SYRUP, THEN SPREAD OVER A THIRD OF THE FILLING. REPEAT THESE LAYERS TWICE MORE. COVER AND LEAVE IN THE FRIDGE TO CHILL OVERNIGHT. LOOSEN FROM THE TIN WITH A KNIFE, THEN REMOVE PAN. SPRINKLE WITH COOKIES AND CANDIED LEMON PEEL, THEN SERVE AND ENJOY!

CRANBERRY MOSCOW MULE GINGERSNAPS

PREP TIME: 20 MINS **COOK TIME:** 11 MINS **SERVES:** 24

DELICIOUSLY SOFT AND CAKEY, THESE COOKIES ARE FULL OF VODKA-INFUSED CRANBERRIES.

FOR THE MIXTURE :

- 135G | 4.75 OZ SWEETENED DRIED CRANBERRIES
- 120ML | 4 OZ VODKA
- 210G | 7.5 OZ ALL-PURPOSE FLOUR
- 2 TSP GROUND GINGER
- 1 TSP GROUND CINNAMON
- 1 TSP BAKING POWDER
- 1/2 TSP KOSHER SALT
- 180G | 6.3 OZ POWDERED SUGAR
- 220G | 7.8 OZ PACKED DARK BROWN SUGAR
- 85G | 3 OZ UNSALTED BUTTER, MELTED
- 60ML | 2 OZ GINGER SYRUP
- 1 TBSP GRATED LIME ZEST FROM 2 LIMES
- 1 TBSP GRATED PEELED FRESH GINGER
- 2 LARGE EGGS

METHOD

STEP 1 IN A MICROWAVEABLE BOWL, ADD THE CRANBERRIES AND THE VODKA, PRESSING DOWN TO SUBMERGE. MICROWAVE FOR 45 SECONDS TO 1 MIN. COVER THE BOWL WITH PLASTIC WRAP TIGHTLY, AND STAND FOR ABOUT 10 MINS UNTIL CRANBERRIES ARE PLUMP. DRAIN THE CRANBERRIES, RESERVING THE VODKA, AND SET ASIDE.

STEP 2 IN A MEDIUM BOWL, WHISK TOGETHER THE FLOUR, GROUND GINGER, CINNAMON, BAKING POWDER, AND SALT.

STEP 3 IN A LARGE BOWL, BEAT TOGETHER THE BROWN SUGAR, BUTTER, GINGER SYRUP, LIME ZEST, AND GRATED FRESH GINGER, UNTIL SMOOTH AND WELL COMBINED. WHISK IN THE FLOUR MIXTURE, THEN FOLD IN THE CRANBERRIES UNTIL EVENLY SPREAD IN THE MIXTURE. COVER THE DOUGH AND PUT IN THE FRIDGE FOR AT LEAST 4 HOURS.

STEP 4 PREHEAT OVEN TO 205 C / 400 F. IN A BOWL, PLACE THE POWDERED SUGAR. USE A 1 1/2-INCH COOKIE OR ICE CREAM SCOOP TO DROP OUT A DOUGH BALL INTO THE SUGAR, AND COAT. PUT THE BALL ON A BAKING SHEET LINED WITH PARCHMENT. REPEAT, LEAVING 2 INCHES BETWEEN EACH BALL. BAKE FOR 9 TO 11 MINUTES, UNTIL PUFFED AND LIGHTLY BROWNED. COOL FOR 2 MINS THEN MOVE TO WIRE RACK. SERVE EITHER WARM OR COOLED. ENJOY!

WHISKEY CRUMBLE MINCE PIES

PREP TIME: 20 MINS **COOK TIME:** 40 MINS **SERVES:** 12

ADD A WHISKEY AND CRUMBLE TWIST TO YOUR USUAL MINCE PIES THIS CHRISTMAS!

FOR THE PASTRY:

- 275G | 9.7 OZ PLAIN FLOUR
- 50G | 1.8 OZ GROUND ALMONDS
- 100G | 3.5 OZ GOLDEN CASTER SUGAR
- 200G | 7 OZ UNSALTED BUTTER, CUBED AND CHILLED
- 1 EGG
- 2 TBSP WHOLE MILK (OPTIONAL)

FOR THE FILLING:

- 500G | 17.6 OZ MINCEMEAT
- 2 TBSP STEM GINGER, ROUGHLY CHOPPED
- ZEST OF 1 ORANGE
- 50G | 1.8 OZ DRIED CRANBERRIES
- 50G | 1.8 OZ GLACÉ MORELLO CHERRIES, ROUGHLY CHOPPED
- 3 TBSP WHISKEY
- 1 EGG, BEATEN
- POWDERED SUGAR, TO DUST

FOR THE CRUMBLE:

- 25G | 0.9 OZ UNSALTED BUTTER, CUBED AND CHILLED
- 50G | 1.8 OZ OATS
- 25G | 0.9 OZ PLAIN FLOUR
- 20G | 0.7 OZ GOLDEN CASTER SUGAR
- 50G | 1.8 OZ PECANS, FINELY CHOPPED

METHOD ♡

STEP 1 IN A FOOD PROCESSOR, ADD ALL OF THE PASTRY INGREDIENTS WITH A PINCH OF SALT AND PULSE UNTIL IT FORMS A DOUGH. ADD SPLASHES OF MILK IF NEEDED. TRANSFER TO A LIGHTLY FLOURED WORKSURFACE, ROLL INTO A SAUSAGE, CUT OFF 1/3 FOR THE LIDS, THEN WRAP AND CHILL IN THE FRIDGE.

STEP 2 WITH THE REST OF THE PASTRY, DIVIDE INTO 12 EQUAL PIECES. ROLL THEM OUT, THEN PRESS INTO A 12-HOLE MUFFIN TIN. CHILL IN THE FRIDGE.

STEP 3 PREHEAT THE OVEN TO 220 C / 430 F. IN A BOWL, MIX THE MINCEMEAT, STEM GINGER, ORANGE ZEST, CRANBERRIES, CHERRIES, AND WHISKEY, THEN DIVIDE OUT INTO THE PASTRY CASES. TAKE THE 1/3 RESERVED PASTRY, ROLL OUT ON A LIGHTLY FLOURED WORK SURFACE AND CUT OUT STARS FOR THE LIDS. CHILL BOTH THE LIDS AND MINCE PIES.

STEP 4 ADD THE BUTTER, OATS, AND FLOUR INTO A BOWL, RUB TOGETHER WITH YOUR FINGERS TO FORM A BREADCRUMB TEXTURE. POUR IN THE SUGAR AND THE PECANS, THEN COMBINE. SPRINKLE THE CRUMBLE OVER THE MINCE PIES, PUT THE STARS ON TOP. BRUSH WITH BEATEN EGG, THEN BAKE FOR 20 MINS. ALLOW TO COOL FOR 15 MINS, THEN DUST WITH POWDERED SUGAR. SERVE AND ENJOY!

BLACKBERRY BABA WITH SPICED CREAM

PREP TIME: 50 MINS **COOK TIME:** 45 MINS **SERVES:** 12

ELEVATE YOUR FRUITY SPONGE CAKE WITH THIS SPIRITED RECIPE!

FOR THE CAKE:

- 70G | 2.5 OZ SOFT BUTTER
- EXTRA BUTTER FOR GREASING THE TIN
- 7G | 2 OZ SACHET FAST-ACTION DRIED YEAST
- 10G | 0.35 OZ HONEY
- 5 MEDIUM EGGS
- 1 TSP GROUND GINGER
- 80G | 2.8 OZ SELF-RAISING FLOUR
- 80G | 2.8 OZ PLAIN FLOUR
- 40G | 1.4 OZ FRESH WHITE BREADCRUMBS

FOR THE SYRUP:

- 200ML | 6.8 OZ OF YOUR FAVORITE SPIRIT (POIRE WILLIAMS, DARK RUM, BRANDY, OR CALVADOS)
- 200G | 7 OZ CASTER SUGAR

FOR THE CREAM:

- 200ML | 6.8 OZ DOUBLE CREAM
- 65G | 2.3 OZ CASTER SUGAR
- 1 TSP GROUND MACE

FOR THE COMPOTE:

- 300G | 10.5 OZ BLACKBERRIES
- 50G | 1.8 OZ CASTER SUGAR
- 1 TBSP LIQUOR (USE THE SAME ONE AS FOR THE SYRUP)

METHOD

STEP 1 MIX ALL OF THE DOUGH INGREDIENTS TOGETHER IN A MIXER WITH A DOUGH HOOK ATTACHMENT. 6-8 MINS ON HIGH SHOULD FULLY COMBINE THE BUTTER AND MAKE A LOOSE BATTER. COVER THE BOWL WITH PLASTIC WRAP AND LEAVE TO PROVE UNTIL DOUBLED IN SIZE (AROUND 30 MINS).

STEP 2 PREHEAT THE OVEN TO 170 C / 340 C AND GREASE A BUNDT TIN. TRANSFER THE MIXTURE TO THE TIN, THEN LEAVE FOR 30 MINS. BAKE FOR 30 MINS IN THE OVEN, UNTIL A STICK COMES OUT CLEAN. TURN OUT TO A WIRE RACK AND ALLOW TO COOL.

STEP 3 MEANWHILE, IN A SAUCEPAN BOIL THE BRANDY, SUGAR AND 200ML / 7 OZ WATER TOGETHER FOR 5 MINS. ONCE THE CAKE HAS COOLED, RETURN TO THE TIN AND DRIZZLE THE HOT SYRUP OVER, LEAVING IT TO SOAK FOR 5-10 MINS.

STEP 4 PUT THE BERRIES, SUGAR AND BRANDY IN A SAUCEPAN OVER A MEDIUM HEAT, STIRRING UNTIL THE BERRIES START TO RELEASE THEIR JUICES. REMOVE AND ALLOW TO COOL.

STEP 5 TO MAKE THE CREAM, WHISK TOGETHER THE CREAM, SUGAR, AND MACE UNTIL SOFT PEAKS FORM. PLACE THE SOAKED SPONGE ON A LARGE PLATE AND SPOON THE BERRIES INTO THE MIDDLE. DOLLOP THE CREAM ON TOP, TOP WITH SOME EXTRA BERRIES, THEN SERVE! ENJOY!

PIÑA COLADA TART

PREP TIME: 45 MINS **COOK TIME:** 55 MINS **SERVES:** 8

DO YOU LIKE PIÑA COLADAS? THEN THIS TROPICAL TART IS FOR YOU.

FOR THE PIE:

- 250G | 8.8 OZ PLAIN FLOUR
- EXTRA FLOUR FOR DUSTING
- 75G | 2.6 OZ POWDERED SUGAR
- 125G | 4.4 OZ UNSALTED BUTTER, CUBED
- 2 EGG YOLKS

FOR THE SYRUP:

- 5 EGGS
- 140G | 5 OZ CASTER SUGAR
- 150ML | 5.1 OZ DOUBLE CREAM
- 80ML | 2.7 OZ PINEAPPLE JUICE (NOT FROM CONCENTRATE)
- 2 SMALL LEMONS, JUICED

FOR THE FILLING:

- 300ML | 10.1 OZ DOUBLE CREAM
- 100ML | 3.4 OZ COCONUT RUM
- MARASCHINO CHERRIES, TO GARNISH
- COCKTAIL UMBRELLAS, TO GARNISH

METHOD

STEP 1 MAKE THE PASTRY BY PUTTING THE FLOUR AND POWDERED SUGAR IN A BOWL, THEN MIXING. RUB IN THE BUTTER USING YOUR FINGERS UNTIL IT IS A BREADCRUMB-LIKE CONSISTENCY. MIX IN THE EGG YOLKS, ADDING 2 TBSP OF WATER IF THE PASTRY IS STILL TOO DRY. FORM THE DOUGH INTO A BALL, FLATTEN TO A DISC, WRAP IN PLASTIC WRAP, THEN CHILL IN THE FRIDGE FOR 30 MINS.

STEP 2 MEANWHILE, MIX ALL OF THE PINEAPPLE FILLING INGREDIENTS TOGETHER IN A BOWL. ROLL THE PASTRY OUT TO ABOUT 1/8 OF AN INCH ON A LIGHTLY FLOURED SURFACE, THEN MOVE TO A 9-INCH TART TRAY, PRESSING DOWN ON THE BOTTOM AND SIDES. CUT OFF THE EXCESS WITH A KNIFE, POKE THE BASE WITH A FORK AND LEAVE AGAIN TO CHILL FOR HALF AN HOUR.

STEP 3 PREHEAT THE OVEN TO 160 C / 320 F. CRUMPLE SOME BAKING PARCHMENT, RE-SMOOTH, THEN LINE THE TART. HOLD DOWN WITH BAKING BEANS OR RICE. BAKE IN THE OVEN FOR 10 MINS, THEN REMOVE THE PARCHMENT AND BEANS, AND BAKE FOR ANOTHER 20 MINS.

STEP 4 ADD THE PINEAPPLE MIXTURE INTO THE PASTRY, LEAVING A SMALL GAP AT THE TOP. BAKE FOR ANOTHER 25 MINS. REMOVE FROM THE OVEN, LEAVE TO COOL, THEN REMOVE FROM TIN AND CHILL FOR 30 MINS.

STEP 5 IN A LARGE BOWL, WHISK TOGETHER THE DOUBLE CREAM AND COCONUT RUM UNTIL THICK. PLOP ON TOP OF THE TART, THEN GARNISH WITH CHERRIES AND COCKTAIL UMBRELLAS. ENJOY!

MADE WITH
LOVE
X

CAKE
SWEETS
SAY
yes